Our Baptist Story

OUR
BAPTIST STORY

Pope A. Duncan

Convention Press

NASHVILLE   TENNESSEE

Printed in the United States of America
25. MY 57 R.R.D.

087576

About the Author

AMONG the numerous eighteenth century Baptist preachers imprisoned in Virginia for "exhorting," there was one Thomas Maxwell. Later he moved to Georgia. He was by no means the last of the Baptist preachers in his line of descent, and many preachers and many generations later the author of this book was born to one of these.

Thus Pope A. Duncan, named for his preacher father, had little chance of escaping being a Baptist minister though he ran from it long enough to get the B.S. and M.S. degrees from the University of Georgia in physics. In due time, however, he attended Southern Baptist Theological Seminary where he earned a Th.D. degree in church history, as his father had done before him.

Apart from a student pastorate and several interim pastorates, his ministry has been spent in teaching. After being thus employed for several years at Mercer University and Stetson University, he went, in 1953, to teach church history in the Southeastern Baptist Theological Seminary at Wake Forest, North Carolina. He resides there with his wife and children.

Contents

CHAPTER 1 OUTLINE

I. ENGLISH BACKGROUND
    1. Seventeenth Century England
    2. General and Particular Baptists

II. THE FIRST BAPTISTS IN AMERICA
    1. Roger Williams
    2. John Clarke

III. FURTHER PLANTINGS
    1. Baptists in New England
    2. Baptists in the Middle Colonies
    3. The First Association in America
    4. Baptists in the South

IV. HEALTHY GROWTH
    1. The Great Awakening
    2. Rise of Separate Baptists

V. STRUGGLE FOR FREEDOM

VI. MISSIONARY INTEREST AND INCREASING CO-OPERATION
    1. Early Missionary Endeavors
    2. American Board of Commissioners for Foreign Missions
    3. The Organization of the Triennial Convention

1

Beginnings in America

ON A SPRING DAY in 1814, four men presented to their fellow delegates the draft of a constitution for a missionary convention which later became the first national organization of Baptists in America. The spring day was Friday, May 20. The four men were Richard Furman of Charleston, Thomas Baldwin of Boston, Stephen Gano of Providence, and William White of Philadelphia. The constitution, adopted the next day, provided "a plan for eliciting, combining, and directing the energies of the whole denomination in one sacred effort, for sending the glad tidings of Salvation to the Heathen, and to nations destitute of pure Gospel-light."

Since the convention met once every three years, it was popularly known as the Triennial Convention, but its official designation was the General Missionary Convention of the Baptist Denomination in the United States of America for Foreign Missions.

This convention was the organization by which Baptists throughout the country carried on their foreign missionary endeavors for thirty-one years. It was strongly supported in both the North and the South. A southerner, Richard Furman, was its first president, and a northerner, Francis Wayland, was the last president before the withdrawal of Southern Baptists. When the

Southern Baptist Convention was organized in 1845, the preamble and much of the flavor of the Triennial Convention's constitution were retained. The General Convention was thus as much the parent of the Southern Baptist Convention as it was of the general missionary bodies of the North.

Now, to be sure, the child is often different in many respects from the parents. Nevertheless, to know and understand the child fully, a knowledge of his ancestry is important. It is no less important, if we are to understand the Southern Baptist Convention, to know something about its origin.

I. ENGLISH BACKGROUND

The Triennial Convention itself did not originate in a vacuum. The Baptist movement, which by 1814 was quite prominent on the American scene, had been represented on these shores since the early seventeenth century. Since the days of Roger Williams, a rather constant, though small, stream of reinforcements from England and Wales had been pouring into the New World.

1. Seventeenth Century England

Seventeenth century England was a land of change and turmoil. Politically there were the Civil War, Cromwell, William and Mary, and the Glorious Revolution. Socially there was the beginning of the assertion of the rights of the common man. Economically there were the beginnings of industrial and economic pre-eminence. Culturally there were Shakespeare, Milton, and the rabid and ribald authors of doggerel verse. But, most of all, the turmoil in England was religious. The Reformation of the established church had occurred in the sixteenth century. However, many believed that the English Reformation achieved too little. There was therefore much discussion in the seventeenth century, resulting in dissenting groups, or sects, of which the largest were the Congregationalists, the Baptists, and the Quakers.

2. General and Particular Baptists

Baptists in England were divided into two principal groups according to their view of Christ's atonement for man's sins. General Baptists preached that he died for all men, Particular Baptists followed Calvin in saying that Christ died for the elect only. In spite of their theological differences, General and Particular Baptists were at one in their practice of believers' baptism, congregational church government, and in their strong appeals for religious liberty. Both groups suffered considerable persecution and many decided to leave the mother country and, in search of freedom, migrate to the American colonies. Though there was a great deal of religious freedom to be had in England during the period of the Commonwealth and Protectorate, there was no permanent peace for dissenters until the Act of Toleration in 1689 under William and Mary. Even this act did not give complete freedom to dissenters though it did permit them to worship freely and to propagate their opinions.

II. THE FIRST BAPTISTS IN AMERICA

1. Roger Williams

Though many came from Britain to the colonies as Baptists, others like Roger Williams became Baptists only after they migrated to the colonies. Williams was a

Cambridge University man. Before he left England to escape the persecution of the intolerant Archbishop Laud, he had become a Puritan with definite Separatist leanings. Though he was welcomed in Boston on his arrival in the winter of 1630–31, he declined to accept a call to the Boston church because he regarded that church as still unseparated from the Anglican establishment. Instead, he became teacher of the church at Salem because he believed it had fully renounced any ties to the Anglican establishment. In time his advanced views regarding democratic church government and the separation of church and state led to his banishment from Massachusetts. Fleeing, before the authorities had opportunity to ship him back to England, he spent many dangerous days in the wilderness areas of that part of New England during the winter of 1635–36. Indians whom he had before befriended now befriended him. Purchasing some land from the Indians, he became the founder of Providence and the Rhode Island Colony.

Williams was a restless person. His mind was ever searching for more truth. This led him to accept some Baptist doctrines, and to submit to baptism in March, 1639, by Ezekiel Holliman. He then baptized Holliman and a few others to form what many call the first Baptist church in North America. After a short time he withdrew from the church and became a Seeker, as he then called himself.

2. John Clarke

Williams' life as a Baptist was so brief that he can have hardly more than symbolic worth as the founder of American Baptists. A friend and compatriot of his,

John Clarke (1609–76), is perhaps due more credit so far as the establishment of early Baptist strength in New England is concerned. Clarke was an Englishman, but he was educated at the University of Leyden, Holland. Like Williams, he sympathized with Puritan views and went to Boston in 1637. There the intolerance of the authorities shocked him, as it did many of the dissenters. He and some friends soon left Boston for Providence where they found religious freedom and a sympathetic spirit in Williams. He helped them settle on the island of Aquidneck which they purchased from the Indians in 1638. The next year Newport was founded. Though there is considerable debate among historians as to the year, it appears that by 1644 Clarke and the church in Newport of which he was pastor were Baptists.

Clarke was equally as forthright in his demands for religious freedom as Roger Williams. In 1651, he went with Williams to England to secure the rights of Rhode Island, and to make certain that no religious tests should ever be put upon those who lived in that colony. While abroad he wrote *Ill Newes from New-England: or a Narrative of New England's Persecution.* This little book constitutes one of the finest defenses of religious liberty written by an American colonist.

III. FURTHER PLANTINGS

1. *Baptists in New England*

In spite of the fact that New England did not provide a fruitful soil for Baptists, there were soon small groups in all of the New England colonies. The opposition of the authorities in most of the colonies led to almost constant harassment of the Baptists. Henry Dunster was forced to resign as president of Harvard because of his Baptist views. John Clarke was fined in the court at Boston, and Obadiah Holmes was imprisoned and whipped for having preached against infant baptism. However, all such efforts to eradicate the Baptist witness failed for little by little the Baptist idea of religious liberty took root in the American mind.

2. *Baptists in the Middle Colonies*

While the growth of Baptists in New England was slow and beset by many difficulties, in the Middle Colonies the situation was quite different. Here the environment was favorable to such groups as Baptists, Quakers, and other dissenters. Here no state church dominated the situation as Congregationalism did in New England or as Anglicanism did in most of the South. Most of the churches in this area seem to have originated around groups of men who had been Baptists previous to their migration to the colonies. Most of them were English, but some Welsh and Irish Baptists were present.

3. *The First Association in America*

Several small churches in the vicinity of Philadelphia in the latter part of the seventeenth century began to strengthen their ties of fellowship through periodic meetings. In 1707, these gatherings culminated in the formation of the first Baptist association in America, the Philadelphia Baptist Association. The five small churches which were involved used a plan of organization which had been employed in England for some years. It did not claim the authority to bind the member churches, but from the very first the association played a major role in settling disputes, giving advice, acting sometimes as a council for ordination or discipline of ministers, and in giving guidance generally in matters of doctrine and polity.

The Philadelphia Association gave a Calvinistic direction to the Baptists of the Middle colonies. In 1742 it adopted the London Confession of Particular Baptists of 1689 with minor changes as its own statement of faith. This Philadelphia Confession, as it is known, became one of the most influential statements of Baptist doctrine and polity ever made in America.

The Philadelphia Association became the mother of many churches and, through itinerant missionaries, made itself felt all up and down the Atlantic seaboard.

4. Baptists in the South

The first Baptist church established in the South was, as far as is known, the First Baptist Church, Charleston, South Carolina. Its founder was William Screven, and he organized it maybe as early as 1683, and not later than 1695. It is barely possible that the 1683 date was for a Baptist church at Somerton, not far from Charleston. It is certainly known that there were Baptists in South Carolina by 1693, that Screven reached Charleston not later than 1696, and that there was a Baptist church in Charleston by 1699.

Whatever the facts are concerning the date and the founder of the church at Charleston, its claim as the first Baptist church in the South is secure. Throughout the colonial period and well into the national period, the church at Charleston was one of the most influential in the South. As the Philadelphia Association was later to do, the Charleston church, in 1700, adopted the London Confession of 1689 as its confession. This action put it clearly in the Calvinist tradition. The same church, led by its pastor, Oliver Hart, recently from the Philadelphia Association, procured the co-operation of three other churches in forming the Charleston Baptist Association, October 21, 1751, the first association in the South and the second in the country.

IV. HEALTHY GROWTH

1. *The Great Awakening*

Revival never comes too soon. Colonial America in the early part of the eighteenth century was far from being the ideal place that it has sometimes been pictured. If the contemporary records are to be believed, immorality of all types abounded, and the churches found tasks most difficult because of apathy and sometimes downright hostility. Beginning between 1725 and 1750, and continuing for many years, there were great and prolonged religious revivals throughout the Colonies. They are called the Great Awakening by historians. Some of the leaders became famous, among them Jonathan Edwards, George Whitfield, William Tennent, and his son, George Tennent.

Baptists were not as intimately involved in the early stages of the Great Awakening as were some other groups, particularly the Presbyterians and the Congregationalists. In New England the majority of their churches were General Baptist churches. Naturally, they did not sympathize with the Calvinistic, predestinarian, character of the revivals. Nevertheless, it was not long before the revival spirit passed to many Baptist churches.

2. Rise of Separate Baptists

Baptists profited from the revival in another and rather unusual way. The Congregational churches had ceased emphasizing the necessity of an experience of regeneration for membership as in previous years; and, when the revival began once more to insist upon personal regeneration, some Congregationalists began to look with favor upon the Baptist emphasis at this point, particularly as it was symbolized in the baptism of believers. As a result, many of them became Baptists.

A closely related development had to do with the controversies which arose over the revivalistic methods which were used, particularly the high emotionalism evident in most of the meetings. These controversies resulted in the schism of many Congregationalist churches into the New Lights who favored the revival and the Old Lights who opposed it. As a result many so-called Separate or strict Congregational churches were organized which insisted upon a personal experience of regeneration for membership. Quite often the separate churches contained both pedobaptists, who practiced infant baptism, and antipedobaptists, who opposed it. In numerous cases these separatist churches became convinced that the New Testament taught either the baptism of infants or sprinkling as baptism. They therefore became Baptist churches. So there developed a group of churches known as Separate churches, as over against the older Baptist churches which were called Regular Baptist churches.

Separate Baptists usually employed a highly emotional type of evangelistic preaching, appealing particularly to the poor and less well-educated, were intense individualists who looked with some suspicion upon any tendency toward associational authority over the churches, and normally would not adhere to the Philadelphia Confession of Faith but insisted upon the Bible alone as their creed. The Separate Baptists were highly successful, particularly as they pushed south under the preaching of such men as Shubael Stearns, Daniel Marshall, and Samuel Harriss. Nevertheless, by the early part of the nineteenth century, Separate and Regular Baptists had united their efforts in most areas.

V. Struggle for Freedom

Baptists, more than any other group, insisted upon religious freedom. Toleration was not enough. They insisted on freedom, not toleration. Rather than merely the concession of the right to exist, religious liberty involves also the right to express one's views in public through any and all means of communication. It involves one's right to proclaim his views freely in order to persuade others to embrace them. It means that no disability shall ever be placed upon a person by the state on account of his religious beliefs and connections. It means that all stand in the same relation to the law regardless of their religion or lack of it. The early seventeenth century British Baptist, Thomas Helwys, had said that the king might punish any person for temporal offenses; yet, for spiritual error, "Let them be heretikes, Turks, Jews or whatsoever, it apperteynes not to the earthy power to punish them in the least measure."

American Baptists were no less hesitant than their British cousins to express the same opinions. From Roger Williams and John Clarke through James Manning, John Gano, Isaac Backus, and John Leland to the present, there has been a continuous and vigorous witness to principles of religious freedom. In colonial days Baptists were almost constantly harassed in New England and in Virginia, but in the other colonies of the South and in the Middle Colonies they had relatively little difficulty. The first association of Baptists in New England, the Warren Association, was organized in 1767 for the primary purpose of strengthening the fight for religious liberty. Over and again the Warren Association made representation to the general courts of Massachusetts and Connecticut for redress. The association also sent Isaac Backus to lay before the Continental Congress its desire for complete religious liberty.

Almost all of the Baptists supported the Revolution. One of their strongest hopes was that out of it would come religious as well as political freedom. By working with all non-Baptists who wanted religious liberty, they succeeded in disestablishing the Anglican (Episcopal) Church in Virginia and procuring the adoption of the Bill of Rights to the Federal Constitution. The last state church to go was the Congregational Church of Massachusetts in 1833.

VI. MISSIONARY INTEREST AND INCREASING CO-OPERATION

1. *Early Missionary Endeavors*

One of the most significant events in American Baptist history was the organization of foreign mission efforts on a national scale in the Triennial Convention. The immediate cause of this new venture was the felt need for the support of Adoniram Judson, his wife Ann, and Luther Rice, all of whom had become convinced of Baptist views and had received baptism after having arrived in the Far East as Congregational missionaries. A lesser known fact is that missionary interest on the part of Baptists in America had been strong even before this event. America itself was a gigantic mission field. The Philadelphia Association had early in its existence sent out itinerant evangelists as missionaries. Baptists in New England and Virginia had carried on similar activities. The general revival in America which swept through the states and frontier territories in the latter part of the eighteenth and the early part of the nineteenth centuries greatly stimulated Baptists along evangelistic and missionary lines. William Carey and the English Baptist missionary endeavor also became an inspiration to Baptists in this country. Individuals and churches often contributed money to be forwarded through the British Baptist Missionary Society to the missionaries in India. The Massachusetts Baptist Missionary Society was founded in Boston in 1802, and other such societies soon came into existence. They devoted most of their efforts to the evangelization of frontier settlements and work among the Indians and the Negro slaves.

2. *American Board of Commissioners for Foreign Missions*

Baptists in America were by no means the only group interested in missionary activities in the early nineteenth century. In fact, the honor of organizing the first national society in America devoted to foreign missions and of sending the first foreign missionaries went to others in 1810, when the American Board of Commissioners for Foreign Missions was organized by Congregationalists in response to the desire of several young men to go to foreign mission fields. In February, 1812, the Board of Commissioners ordained its first missionaries: Judson, Newell, Nott, Hall, and Rice. In the same month these young men set sail for missionary duty in India.

3. *The Organization of the Triennial Convention*

Judson, knowing that on arrival in India he would come into contact with English Baptist missionaries, undertook a study of the scriptural teachings concerning baptism in order to prepare himself to face the Baptist arguments. To his amazement he became convinced by his study that the Baptists were right. Once in India he was joined in his newly found convictions by his wife Ann and his friend Luther Rice. They now sought and received baptism at the hands of English Baptist missionaries. After this happened, Judson and Rice resigned from their position with the Board of Commissioners and sought help from the Baptists of America. Their appeals found ready response among American Baptists. Judson, in a letter to Dr. Thomas Baldwin, pastor of the First Baptist Church in Boston, had indicated that if Baptists should form a society for the support of a missionary, he would be ready to consider himself their missionary. A few days after Baldwin had received this letter, prayer meetings for missions had begun in Boston, and the Baptist Society for Propagating the Gospel in

India and Other Foreign Parts was soon organized in Baldwin's home. This was to be the society for Massachusetts, and it was thought that other such societies would be organized with which it could join.

It soon became clear that it would be impossible for the Judsons and Rice to serve in India, so they sought another country for their endeavors. Eventually Judson and his wife made their way to Burma to supplement the work of an English Baptist mission station already there under the leadership of William Carey's son, Felix. Since Judson and Rice had no rapid means of communication, they were uncertain about the response of Baptists in America to their appeal. In addition, a severe liver ailment had caused Rice intense suffering, and he needed medical help. It was therefore agreed that Rice would return to America to help develop missionary support among the Baptists.

Rice was a true missionary statesman, and even before landing in America he had envisioned a national missionary society. Immediately upon arrival he plunged into the task of generating enthusiasm. He spent himself unselfishly traveling by any means available up and down the coast visiting churches and associations. Though foreign mission societies like the one which had been organized in Boston sprang up all about, Rice was never satisfied until he could bring the churches to see the necessity of a national agency. Other men had previously tried to get Baptists to co-operate on the national level. It was not, however, until Rice supplied the motive that such an organization appeared.

Rice proposed that a national convention be held in Philadelphia in June, 1814, but it actually met a few weeks earlier, May 18, 1814. Eleven states and Washington, D. C., were represented by thirty-three delegates. All sections were represented, though the Middle States sent the majority of the delegates. Six came from the South, but one of them, Richard Furman of Charleston, was elected president of the convention. The great missionary spirit, Thomas Baldwin, was made secretary. The adoption of a constitution by the delegates, creating the Triennial Convention, has already been mentioned. The constitution also set up the Baptist Board of Foreign Missions in the United States composed of twenty-one commissioners to act for the convention between sessions.

For the first time the word "convention" appears in the title of the organization of American Baptists. In addition, the organization was of a general character; the whole denomination was included. Rice and Judson, who became the first missionaries of this new body, had made a contribution perhaps far beyond their own power to comprehend.

SUGGESTED TOPICS FOR DISCUSSION

1. Discuss the circumstances which led to the organization of the first association in America.
2. Discuss the relationship of the Great Awakening to Baptist advance.
3. Discuss the circumstances which brought a national organization of Baptists into being.

I. EARLY VIRGINIA BAPTISTS
   1. General Baptists
   2. Particular (Regular) Baptists
   3. Separate Baptists
   4. Persecution of Baptists

II. BAPTIST BEGINNINGS IN MARYLAND

III. BAPTISTS IN THE CAROLINAS
   1. Beginnings in North Carolina
   2. Separate Baptists in South Carolina

IV. BAPTIST BEGINNINGS IN GEORGIA

V. EARLY SUCCESSES IN KENTUCKY AND TENNESSEE
   1. Beginnings in Kentucky
   2. The Great Kentucky Revival
   3. Beginnings in Tennessee

VI. BAPTISTS ON THE MOVE
   1. Missouri
   2. Mississippi and Louisiana
   3. Alabama
   4. Florida
   5. Arkansas
   6. Texas

VII. REVOLUTION AND FREEDOM

VIII. STRIDES IN EDUCATION
   1. Early Efforts to Secure an Educated Ministry
   2. The Work of Oliver Hart
   3. The Leadership of Richard Furman and the Charleston Association
   4. The Organization of Furman Academy and Theological Institute
   5. Other Early Educational Institutions

IX. CONTROVERSY AND DIVISION
   1. The Anti-Effort Secession
   2. The Schism of Alexander Campbell

2

Baptists in Dixie Land

WHEN South Carolina seceded from the Union, December 20, 1860, she was merely exerting a leadership in the South which she had exercised in most respects for many years. Her leadership among Baptists of the South had long been established.

Some time in the last two decades of the seventeenth century, the first Baptist church in the South had been established at or near Charleston. The first association in Dixie had appeared in South Carolina in 1751. This Charleston Association, in 1821, was also instrumental in helping to bring together delegates to organize the first state Baptist convention in the United States. Baptist beginnings in education in the South can also be found in South Carolina. The Furman Academy and Theological Institution first opened its doors in January, 1827. Therefore, it is no surprise to find that a South Carolinian, William Bullein Johnson, who had served as president of the Triennial Convention, became the first president of the Southern Baptist Convention at its formation in 1845, and that when the Southern Baptist Theological Seminary began in 1859, it was located at Greenville, South Carolina.

Though South Carolina exerted a significant leadership among Baptists in the South before the organization of the Southern Baptist Convention, the Baptists in the other Southern states were active and rapidly increasing in numbers and influence.

I. EARLY VIRGINIA BAPTISTS

1. *General Baptists*

The first Baptists of record in Virginia were General Baptists who evidently had come directly from England. The first mention of them is in January, 1699, when an English Quaker visiting Virginia wrote that a meeting of Friends had been held at the house of a General Baptist preacher at "York City." These Baptists, no doubt, were few in number and without significant influence.

In response to an appeal from a group of General Baptists in Virginia, the general assembly of the General Baptists of England in 1714 sent two men to help their brethren. Of these two only Robert Norden survived the voyage across the Atlantic. It appears that Norden exercised a helpful leadership among these Baptists until his death in 1725.

The future of Baptist life in Virginia was not to be with General Baptists, however; and by the middle of the eighteenth century their churches in Virginia were moving toward extinction.

2. *Particular (Regular) Baptists*

Another stream of Baptist life in Virginia received its original strength from a group of General Baptist people who migrated from Maryland to the western part of the state in 1743. A church was soon organized in what is now Berkeley County, West Virginia. Not long after, the church found itself in need of assistance and advice and applied for help to the Philadelphia Association. The church at Ketocton had also been constituted, and now the Philadelphia Association responded to both and sent four men to assist, one of them being John Gano (1727–1804), who was a prominent Baptist and a chaplain in the Revolutionary Army who often had General Washington in his audience. One result was that the General (Arminian) Baptists greatly declined in the area and the Regular (Calvinistic) Baptists multiplied rapidly and became strong.

The churches of Opekon (Mill Creek) and Ketocton were admitted to membership in the Philadelphia Association in 1754, but these churches and others grew so rapidly that by 1766 they formed their own association—the Ketocton.

3. *Separate Baptists*

A third group of Baptists found in Virginia in the colonial period were the Separate Baptists whose origin was referred to in the previous chapter. Daniel Marshall and Shubael Stearns were in the colony as early as 1754. However, Stearns, not happy with the immediate prospects, removed in 1755 to North Carolina. There he had remarkable success, and in 1758 the Sandy Creek Association was formed. From that association a group of young preachers, including Marshall, carried the Baptist witness into adjacent parts of Virginia. One of the most influential converts of this group was Colonel Samuel Harriss (1724–99) who had been a prominent figure in Halifax County. He was soon ordained and became an effective preacher.

The first organized Separate Baptist church in Virginia was the Dan River (1760). It soon put out "branches," and Separate Baptist churches sprang up quickly and spread rapidly.

The Separate Baptists were endowed with the warm emotionalism of the Great Awakening. Their preachers generally had little formal education, though many of them had much native ability. They emphasized man's depravity, Christ's atonement, the need of a conscious new birth, and the immersion of believers. They were often criticised by the more conservative Regular Baptist ministers for their highly emotional preaching by uneducated men, and for the noise and confusion which seemed so often to accompany their meetings. Nevertheless, other Regular Baptists like John Gano saw that, though their practices were somewhat disorderly, they nevertheless were sincere, godly men who were doing a great deal of good.

In the beginning, the churches of the Separate Baptists in Virginia and the Carolinas all belonged to the Sandy Creek Association. In 1770 the association decided to divide itself into three bodies, one for each state. In Virginia the resulting organization in 1771 was the General Association of the Separate Baptists in Virginia, commonly called the Rapidan or Orange Association.

4. Persecution of Baptists

Both Regular and Separate Baptists had to bear misrepresentation, personal mistreatment, and mob violence. In time legal means were used in the attempt to suppress the Separate preachers. In June, 1768, John

Waller, Louis Craig, James Chiles, James Read, and Jim Marsh were arraigned as disturbers of the peace. The prosecuting attorney in his accusation of them said to the court: "May it please your worships, these men are great disturbers of the peace. They cannot meet a man upon the road, but they must ram a text of scripture down his throat." Convicted, Chiles, Craig, and Waller, who were residents of the county, spent some time in jail. Imprisonment and mistreatment of Baptists spread widely in the next few years. Several, like James Ireland, suffered severely. He lay in the one-room jail of Culpepper from November until April, and during this period was almost constantly abused. As a result his health was permanently injured. Only a youth of twenty-one, he bore his suffering with courage, dignity, and serenity. Except for the case of Elijah Baker in 1778, the records of imprisonment ceased after 1774. There yet remained, however, a long struggle in Virginia for complete religious freedom, and in this struggle Baptists played a major role. The suffering which Baptists endured in this period served only to accelerate their growth.

II. Baptists Beginnings in Maryland

Though there was a large amount of religious freedom in Maryland, Baptists were rather slow in organizing churches in that colony and never came to have an exceptionally strong program. The first Baptist church was founded in 1742 at Chestnut Ridge. Henry Sater, an English General Baptist, had settled there as early as 1709, and it was largely through his efforts that the church came into existence. Sater's church thrived and soon busied itself with organizing other churches. Though the first church in Baltimore was not founded until 1785, that city soon became the center of Baptist interest in Maryland.

Separate Baptists seem not to have settled in Maryland. As a consequence, Baptist growth there was much slower than in Virginia and the Carolinas. Baptists were scattered and had little cohesiveness, often being connected with associations in other colonies.

III. BAPTISTS IN THE CAROLINAS

1. *Beginnings in North Carolina*

The story of Baptist beginnings in South Carolina has already been briefly told. The honor of organizing the first Baptist church on record in North Carolina goes to Paul Palmer. Before going to North Carolina, he had preached in the home of Henry Sater, preparing the way for the later organization of the first Baptist church in Maryland. Though Palmer was there by 1720, it was not until 1727 that he was successful in organizing a Baptist church in North Carolina in the Chowan precinct. Unfortunately, it ceased to exist after three or four years.

Even before it disbanded, Palmer was busy spreading the Baptist witness to other parts of the colony. As a result, a church was organized in 1729 at Shiloh in Camden County. This church, unlike the one in Chowan, did not die, and is now the oldest Baptist church in North Carolina. Both of these churches had been organized as General Baptist churches, though later (in 1757) Shiloh was reconstituted as a Particular Baptist church. Like the Shiloh Church, most early Baptist churches in North

Carolina were of the General Baptist persuasion. However, the decade 1750–1760 saw the almost complete transformation of the General Baptists to Particular Baptists. Again the influence of the Philadelphia Association and its remarkable agent, John Gano, were determinative.

Along with the change of the General Baptists to Particular Baptists came the introduction of Separate Baptist views into North Carolina. As has been indicated, the first Separate Baptist church was organized at Sandy Creek in 1755 with Shubael Stearns as the leader. The movement grew with remarkable speed. Within seventeen years, forty-two churches had grown out of the mother church. Their association, the Sandy Creek, was organized in 1758.

2. *Separate Baptists in South Carolina*

The Separates were also active in South Carolina throughout the middle of the eighteenth century. Daniel Marshall and Philip Mulkey were especially active there. Mulkey's influence was felt for years in the numerous early Baptist churches of the South Carolina back country. When the Sandy Creek Association dismissed the Virginia and South Carolina churches to form their own associations, the South Carolina Separates formed the Congaree Association (1771).

IV. BAPTIST BEGINNINGS IN GEORGIA

There were Baptists in the colony of Georgia from its early days. Some of them had been associated with the churches at Charleston and Euhaw in South Carolina. Though limited efforts had been made to organize regular church life in the colony before, no Baptist church had been successfully constituted until Daniel Marshall, the Separate Baptist, moved from South Carolina in 1771 and settled on Kiokee Creek. Under his leadership the Kiokee Baptist Church was constituted in 1772. Other churches soon sprang up. Twelve years later, when the Georgia Baptist Association was organized (1784), there were still only six churches in the whole state. Within another decade, however, there were fifty-two Baptist churches.

V. EARLY SUCCESSES IN KENTUCKY AND TENNESSEE

The latter part of the eighteenth century and the early nineteenth saw a general revival of religion in the United States. The Baptists of the South were strongly affected by it. The membership of churches increased, new churches sprang up, and spiritual vitality deepened. One of the valuable by-products was the gradual union of Regular and Separate Baptists in the Southeast.

1. *Beginnings in Kentucky*

While the Seaboard states profited greatly by the revival, nowhere were the results more spectacular than in the new frontier areas of Kentucky and Tennessee. Baptists went into Kentucky with the prerevolutionary settlers who crossed the Alleghenies to blaze trails and explore the area. The Boone family was of Baptist stock. Squire Boone, the brother of Daniel Boone, was a Baptist preacher. Though there were occasional preaching services held earlier, the first Baptist church constituted west of the mountains was the Severns Valley Church (June 18, 1781). Many Regular and Separate Baptist churches were organized in the new territory during the 1780's, most of them by immigrants from Virginia and North Carolina. With the recession which occurred in the Seaboard states after the Revolutionary War, a great stream of immigrants, many Baptists among them, crossed the mountains. Occasionally entire churches would move. Perhaps the most famous of these was the church of Louis Craig of Virginia. Craig's church, known as the "Traveling Church," decided in 1781 to move to Kentucky. Almost the entire membership went, keeping up their organization as they traveled, their pastor preaching to them as they camped along the way. By 1785, Baptists were strong enough in the new territory to form an association. On September 30, six churches organized the Elkhorn Association with the Philadelphia Confession of Faith as its standard.

2. *The Great Kentucky Revival*

The real growth of Baptists in this area began, however, with the great revival which swept over the frontier in the earliest years of the nineteenth century. Though the Presbyterians and the Methodists were more directly involved in its origin, Baptists were soon reaping great benefits. High emotionalism attended much of the revival, though Baptists were not given to such excesses as the Presbyterians and the Methodists. Where there were six Kentucky associations, 106 churches, and 5,110 members in 1800, by 1803 there were ten associations, 219 churches, and 15,495 members.

3. *Beginnings in Tennessee*

Before 1775 there were Baptist settlers from Virginia

and North Carolina in Tennessee. These were settled in the valleys in the eastern portions of the territory. The difficult days which came with the opening of the Revolution seem to have broken up the two small Baptist churches which apparently had been formed. Following the war, Glade-Hollows, one of these churches, was reconstituted. By 1780 still other Baptists had moved into the area. One group, coming from the Sandy Creek Church in North Carolina, constituted a church on Boon's Creek. By 1781 five or six churches existed in eastern Tennessee. An independent association was not formed immediately, and until 1786 most of the churches continued a relationship with the Sandy Creek Association. However, in that year seven churches formed the Holston Association. Though there were both Regular and Separate Baptists among these earlier settlers, by the time the association was organized the differences had largely disappeared and the Philadelphia Confession of Faith was adopted.

VI. BAPTISTS ON THE MOVE

1. *Missouri*

Many Baptists of North and South Carolina and Kentucky were intrepid pioneers who continued to push westward. Even while Missouri was still a part of the Louisiana territory, some of them found their way into that region. Living under Spanish and Catholic rule, they were not able to organize their church life, though itinerant preachers did sometimes visit their settlements and hold services. When Missouri became a part of the United States, Baptists, particularly those from Kentucky, began to flood across the border. The Tywappity Church, constituted in 1804 or 1805, was the first Baptist church in the territory and may well have been the first non-Catholic church as well. By 1816 Baptist strength was such that the Bethel Baptist Association was formed. The following year six churches organized the Missouri Baptist Association.

2. *Mississippi and Louisiana*

While this territory was still under Spanish rule, Baptists came from South Carolina and Georgia to live. A Baptist church was formed as early as 1780 in Mississippi. After the territory was ceded to the United States, churches increased so rapidly that by 1806 the Mississippi Baptist Association was organized. The first church in Louisiana, Bayou Chicot, was organized in 1812.

3. *Alabama*

Alabama was relatively late in being settled. There is no record of Baptists in the territory earlier than 1808. These early pioneers came from Tennessee and Georgia. The first church, organized October 2, 1808, was near the present site of Huntsville on the Flint River.

4. *Florida*

Since this territory was so long under the flags of other nations, Baptist work was late beginning. Though there were Baptists and Baptist preachers present earlier, it was not until January, 1821, that the first church was organized at Pigeon Creek in Nassau County. Much of the early work in Florida was done by missionaries from the associations of southern Alabama and southern

Georgia. It was not until 1841 that the Florida Association, the first in the state, was organized.

5. *Arkansas*

Not until 1818 was there any organized Baptist church in Arkansas. It was then that the Salem Church was constituted in what is now Randolph County. The Little Rock Association came into existence in 1824. Early growth was relatively slow.

6. *Texas*

Though there had been some Baptist witness in Texas following the arrival of Joseph Bays from Missouri in 1820, there was no organized Baptist church on Texas soil until Daniel Parker's Pilgrim Church of Predestinarian Regular Baptists entered in 1834. Parker's church held strange doctrines and was antimissionary, but through Parker it had great influence. He found that Mexican colonization laws forbade the organizing of any but a Catholic church in Texas but did not prohibit the immigration of one into the territory. Consequently, he gathered followers and organized them into a church in Illinois and then proceeded to travel with his church into Texas. Missionary Baptists soon moved into the territory, and in 1840 organized the Union Association. By 1843 there were enough missionary Baptist churches to organize the Sabine Association.

VII. REVOLUTION AND FREEDOM

Though Baptists everywhere supported the cause of the American Revolution, they were concerned that the whole field of liberty be cultivated. They felt that religious liberty was essential to political liberty. Consequently, their activities centered largely in this area. By the time of the Revolution, Baptists had become a significant force in the South, and they now renewed their demands for full religious freedom. The Virginia Assembly was flooded with their petitions.

In the South it was the Episcopal Church which was established. Except in Virginia its disestablishment came with relative ease before the end of the war. When the war ended, others joined the Baptists as allies in the struggle for religious liberty. Such statesmen as George Mason, James Madison, Patrick Henry, and Thomas Jefferson had become persuaded of the desirability of religious liberty. The struggle was not finally won until 1785 when Thomas Jefferson's Bill for Establishing Religious Freedom was adopted by the Virginia Assembly. The struggle in Virginia, and the subsequent victory, was significant nationally as a pattern for the Federal Government.

VIII. Strides in Education

1. *Early Efforts to Secure an Educated Ministry*

Baptist growth in the eighteenth century was remarkable. The pastoral leadership of the great mass of people was largely in the hands of uneducated, though earnest and devout, men. Most of them did not see the necessity of undergirding the newly won Baptist strength with an educated leadership and an intelligent organization. Fortunately, however, there were in the South a few educated leaders, and others who were self-educated. These men believed that evangelistic and missionary activities could not long survive or be greatly significant unless supported by a program of Christian education. Working against great odds and much opposition, these men, including such leaders as Richard Furman, W. B. Johnson, W. T. Brantley, Sr., Adiel Sherwood, Jesse Mercer, and Samuel Wait, helped create means for the education of the Baptist people.

Fully equipped educational institutions, long in coming, were preceded by sincere and often successful efforts to educate a rising ministry. The normal pattern at first was for individual churches, associations, or special educational societies to raise funds with which to purchase books and pay the expenses of candidates for the ministry while they studied in the homes of older ministers. From these meager beginnings first academies, and then denominational colleges grew.

2. *The Work of Oliver Hart*

As in so many fields of early Baptist endeavor, South Carolina assumed the leadership here. When in 1750 Oliver Hart of Pennsylvania became pastor of the Charleston Church, South Carolina Baptists had not yet produced a native preacher, though their work was more than fifty years old in Charleston. A man of great vigor and ability who had come under the warm influence of the Great Awakening, Hart by his effective evangelism led in the expansion of the Baptist witness in that area. One result of his ministry was the entrance of several young men into the ministry. Though he was not a well-educated man himself, he realized the importance of education. He had earlier been associated with Isaac Eaton, the founder of the first school in America under

Baptist auspices—Hopewell Academy. Being convinced also from his acquaintance with the leaders of the Philadelphia Association that education added to the preacher's power, he felt it his duty to arrange for the education of these young ministerial candidates. By action of the association in 1755, he and two other ministers were made trustees of an educational fund which was to be raised by the churches to defray at least a part of the expenses of men studying under the direction of older and better educated ministers. Later in 1765, when Rhode Island College (later Brown University), the first Baptist college in America, was founded, it had the support of the leaders of the Charleston Association, including Mr. Hart.

3. The Leadership of Richard Furman and the Charleston Association

The Revolutionary War interrupted many of the plans of the Baptists in the South, including the educational endeavors of the Charleston Association. Hart, driven out of the state by the British, never returned, but his successor, Richard Furman, carried to even greater success the work which Hart began. Under his leadership, a "general committee" was formed by the association to administer the educational funds. Furman, elected president of this committee, served thirty-five years or until his death in 1825.

Though the association, through its committee, helped to support an academy conducted by John M. Roberts and purchased "a complete theological library" for its students, a feeling grew that there should be an educational institution organized under Baptist support and control. The first official note about such a feeling is re-corded in the 1810 minutes of the association.

About this same time the increasing interest of Baptists in foreign missions presented a powerful motive to Baptist organization and to strengthening Baptist educational efforts. Luther Rice, convinced of the necessity for trained ministers both at home and abroad, gave his powerful voice to the cause of Christian education. Richard Furman, president of the new Triennial Convention, was equally as convinced of the need of an expanded educational program. The Triennial Convention itself supported a theological seminary in Philadelphia from 1818 until 1822, when it merged with Columbian College, Washington, D. C. The Charleston Association strongly supported these efforts also.

4. *The Organization of Furman Academy and Theological Institute*

Feelings began to mature among South Carolina Baptists that they should organize a "general association" which would co-operate with the district associations in promoting their educational and missionary interests. Furman, as usual, was a strong advocate of such a procedure. In spite of discouraging circumstances, a state convention was organized in Columbia, December 4, 1821, the first in the South and the third in the nation.

Education was the prime object to be fostered by the state convention. A school was not immediately begun. Many factors caused the delay. One was the possibility and desirability of co-operating with the Georgia Baptist General Association, organized in 1822, but called Convention after 1828. At the convention in 1825 concrete steps were taken toward beginning a school. As a result, Furman Academy and Theological Institution opened at Edgefield in January, 1827. Its early years were full of trial and discouragement, but it blazed a trail, and other states soon organized their own schools.

5. *Other Early Educational Institutions*

Kentucky Baptists procured a charter for Georgetown College in 1829. Many difficulties kept it from having a full faculty and a regular system of classes until 1840.

The Virginia Baptist Education Society was organized in 1830, and a school opened for its beneficiaries that fall. In 1832, the society opened the Virginia Baptist Seminary. The work expanded, and a charter was obtained in 1840 for what had become Richmond College.

Georgia Baptists were fortunate in having such men as Henry Holcombe, Jesse Mercer, W. T. Brantley, Sr., Adiel Sherwood, and Josiah Penfield to promote educational work. Josiah Penfield bequeathed to the Georgia Baptist Convention twenty-five hundred dollars as the basis of a fund for theological education. This stimulated an already active interest in education on the part of such men as Jesse Mercer. After Penfield's death in 1829, a tract of land was purchased in Greene County in 1832. The next year, Mercer Institute was established.

The North Carolina Baptist State Convention, organized in 1830, had as one of its primary objects the education of men called to the ministry. In 1832, a farm was purchased upon which a Baptist educational institution was to be located. However, it was 1834 before Wake Forest Institute opened its doors under the presidency of Samuel Wait. In the beginning the manual labor principle was employed but in a few years it was abandoned and the school's name changed to Wake Forest College.

After the failure of one educational enterprise begun in 1834, the Baptists of Alabama abandoned the matter of education for a number of years. In response to sheer necessity, however, Howard College was organized in 1842. It developed gradually into a leading Baptist institution.

Other schools which were operated by Baptists by the year of the formation of the Southern Baptist Convention were Judson College for women, in Alabama, established 1839; the Western Baptist Theological Institute at Covington, Kentucky, which had a short career; Union University at Murfreesboro, Tennessee; Limestone College in South Carolina; and Baylor University and Mary Hardin Baylor College in Texas. Mississippi College was founded as Hampstead Academy in 1826 by the Presbyterians, but it was not transferred to Baptist control until 1850.

IX. CONTROVERSY AND DIVISION

No movement ever grows or becomes influential without internal tensions and disagreements. Normally these are healthy and lead to proper compromise and solution. However, it sometimes happens that such fundamental issues become matters of controversy, and such intense feelings are generated that much harm is done. Occasionally the only solution is division. In the period before 1845, differences of opinion among Baptists were often found. Most of these were soon overcome. There were, however, three major controversies which resulted in large-scale division. One of these resulted in the formation of the Southern Baptist Convention (see next chapter). The other two, the anti-effort secession and the schism of Alexander Campbell, deserve brief mention here.

1. *The Anti-Effort Secession*

As has been seen, the early years of the nineteenth century brought a revival in Baptist ranks. As a result, Baptists began to engage effectively in home and foreign missions, Sunday school work, education, and other various benevolent enterprises. There soon developed organizations to foster them and to combine the efforts of Baptists in co-operative enterprises. From the beginning, all these activities and organizations met with opposition. It grew in strength and bitterness until by about 1840 those who felt strongly against the promotion of missions and education separated from their brethren and proclaimed themselves to be the Old Side or Primitive Baptists.

The chief leaders of this movement appeared in the frontier area, particularly in the Ohio Valley. They were Daniel Parker, William Thompson, and John Taylor. The influence of these men and of two journals, *The Signs of the Times* and *The Primitive Baptist,* did greatest damage in Kentucky, Tennessee, and north Alabama. Yet, no section entirely escaped the deadening influence of antimission views. Every form of progress was opposed, and any support of the agents of that progress was cause for a breach of fellowship. For example, the following resolution was adopted by the Yellow River Association of Georgia in 1838:

That the institutions of the day, called benevolent, to-wit: The Convention, Bible Society, Sunday School Union, Tract Society, Temperance Society, Abolition Society, Theological Seminary, and all other institutions tributary to the missionary plan, now existing in the United States, are unscriptural, and that we, as an Association, will not correspond with any Association that has united with them; nor will we hold in our communion or fellowship any church that is connected with them.

Several factors combined to bring the anti-effort movement into being and to make it relatively successful. Appalling ignorance on the part of many led to suspicion and distrust of education and educated men. This attitude led naturally to jealousy on the part of untrained ministers toward those who sometimes came among them preaching missions and education. Some were even fearful that missionary societies and schools would drain their people of their money and leave none with which they might be paid. They also feared that the new organizations would assume such authority that the autonomy of the local church would be impaired. Some argued that these new organizations were unscriptural since there was no mention of them in the Bible. A most formidable cause of antimissionism was theological. Some interpreted Calvinism, which emphasized God's election, to mean that God did not require or desire human means in spreading the gospel. This meant that all human effort—missions, Sunday schools, colleges and theological seminaries, and Bible and temperance societies—was not only not needed, but was actually sinful because it stressed human effort as necessary if people were to be won to a saving faith in Christ. One reason for much of the success of the anti-effort Baptists was the difficulty involved in getting information to the people.

This hyper or super-Calvinism undercut every progressive effort, and the opposition arising from it when missionary organizations were in their infancy did much damage because it was difficult to get information to the people.

2. *The Schism of Alexander Campbell*

Troubles come, as proverbial wisdom has said, not singly but in pairs. The first half of the nineteenth century saw Baptists struggling not only with the anti-effort movement, but also with Alexander Campbell and his followers. He and his father, Thomas Campbell, had come out of a conservative Presbyterian background but they had gradually broken with that heritage. They and their followers then organized themselves into the Brush Run Church (May 4, 1811). Previously, Thomas Campbell had formed the Christian Association of Washington and had set forth as the watchword of his followers, "Where the Scriptures speak, we speak; where they are silent, we are silent."

After a time, the Campbells became convinced that believers' baptism by immersion was the only scriptural baptism. The Brush Run Church consequently accepted this view. After some negotiations on both sides, the church applied for membership in the Redstone Baptist Association of Pennsylvania and was accepted in 1813. Alexander Campbell soon became a leading figure in western Tennessee, Kentucky, and western Virginia.

Campbell was a powerful debater, and when he so

clearly won his debate with McCalla, a Presbyterian minister, in a debate at Washington, Kentucky, in 1823, many Baptists looked upon him as their leader. However, some were concerned about his views on baptism which seemed to them to emphasize baptismal regeneration.

In order to propagate his views, Campbell began to publish *The Christian Baptist* in 1823 (replaced in 1829 by *The Millennial Harbinger*). He liked to think of himself as "the Reformer," and his followers as "Reformers." They desired what they called the "restoration of the ancient order of things." It was not long until nearly all the Baptist churches in Kentucky and many in western Virginia and Tennessee had groups of "Reformers" within them. In his publication he frequently opposed missionary societies, ordination, seminaries, Bible societies, and church associations. In Kentucky and Virginia, particularly, whole churches, and sometimes even whole associations, were captured by Campbell. However, strong men opposed Campbell's doctrines and methods. Notable among them were Silas M. Noel of Kentucky and Jeremiah B. Jeter of Virginia. Soon churches, and then associations, began withdrawing fellowship from the "Reformers." By about 1830 most of Campbell's followers were organized in churches separate from the Baptists. Though generally known as Disciples of Christ, they were also sometimes called the Christian Church, a term employed by Barton W. Stone, who with his followers in Kentucky held views similar to those of Campbell. While other denominations lost members to Campbell's movement, Baptists were the greatest losers, losing about ten thousand members in Kentucky alone between the years 1829 and 1831.

In spite of the untold damage which had been done to the Baptists of the South by the anti-effort secessions and the schism of Alexander Campbell, Baptist growth and missionary activity did not cease, but rather grew, and the greatest growth was yet to come.

SUGGESTED TOPICS FOR DISCUSSION

1. Discuss the significance of the consolidation of Regular and Separate Baptists.
2. Discuss Baptist contributions to religious liberty in America.
3. Discuss the significance of education and missions to Baptist growth.

CHAPTER 3 OUTLINE

I. THE PATH TO SEPARATION
   1. The Lack of Focus for a Denominational Consciousness
   2. The "Society" Versus the "Convention" Method
   3. Complaints Against the American Baptist Home Mission Society
   4. The Primary Problem of Slavery
   5. The Crisis

II. THE CONVENTION IS FORMED
   1. The Virginia Baptist Foreign Mission Society Issues the Call
   2. The First Meeting of the Convention
   3. The Convention's Constitution

III. A NEW ERA BEGINS

3

Division Among Brethren

BRETHREN sometimes have to agree to disagree. Occasionally, when they find their disagreement hindering their work, they may agree to dissolve their union and pursue their endeavors separately. In such a spirit the parting of the ways came to Baptists in America in 1845 when the Baptists of the South organized the Southern Baptist Convention. Good friends and sincere men like Francis Wayland of the North and Richard Fuller of the South found themselves unable to agree on the matter of slavery. In their correspondence, published early in 1845 under the title *Letters on Domestic Slavery*, these two men debated the slavery question in as courteous and considerate a spirit as the circumstances would allow.

When separation appeared to be the only possible course, many men in the North saw the logic of it and felt like Wayland, who wrote J. B. Jeter: "You will separate of course. I could not ask otherwise. . . . Put away all violence, act with dignity and firmness, and the world will approve your course."

I. THE PATH TO SEPARATION

The causes of major events are seldom simple, and are usually more complex than they appear on the surface.

The causes which led to the formation of the Southern Baptist Convention were no exception to this general rule. Though differences over slavery was the most obvious, and certainly the most significant cause, other causes were there, though they were less easily perceived and more difficult to understand.

1. *The Lack of Focus for a Denominational Consciousness*

In a large country like the United States sectional differences arise in denominations as well as in political parties. The preceding paragraphs referred to some of the differences arising from sectional interests and viewpoints relating to slavery. A second difference, not so urgent but nevertheless deep-seated, concerned organized denominational life. In the North the emphasis was upon independent societies for carrying on various phases of denominational work, self-governing societies that looked primarily to individuals, certainly at first, for support. In the South a conviction developed that both on the state and the national level there should be conventions with power to set up and direct various kinds of missionary, educational, and benevolent work through boards, and so have a centralized and effective denominational program for developing co-operation and building a strong denominational rather than society loyalty.

What occurred in the North was the development of societies instead of a convention. The Triennial Convention, popularly so called because it met only once every three years, was in reality a society, as its name indicates: the General Missionary Convention of the United States of America for Foreign Missions. (It was organized at Philadelphia in May, 1814, but later located at Boston.) For only a very short period did it do home mission work or promote education through Columbian College, Washington, D.C. (now an independent institution, George Washington University.) A year after the formation of the Southern Baptist Convention it changed its name to the American Baptist Missionary Union. It is known today as the American Baptist Foreign Missionary Society.

The American Baptist Home Mission Society was organized at New York City in 1832. It was an independent society. The Baptist General Tract Society was organized at Washington, D.C., in February, 1824, but was moved to Philadelphia a few years later to become the American Baptist Publication Society in 1844. It was also an independent society.

Because of disagreements with the American Bible Society (organized May, 1816) over translation work, the Baptists organized the American and Foreign Bible Society (provisional, May 13, 1836; permanent, April 26, 1837). Because of further difficulties that arose, another predominantly Baptist Bible society, the American Bible Union, was organized June 10, 1850. Both of these were independent societies. They were merged into the American Baptist Publication Society in 1883.

There was no general Baptist organization to which all of these societies were responsible. Each, independent of the others, had its own annual session. Before long they agreed on a general time for their annual meetings, with one following the other in the same city, so that a member of any society could, if he wished, attend all of them. Some belonged to two or more of the societies because they gave money for their support. One can easily see how all of these independent societies made it impossible for the denomination to have a centralized and effective program for developing denominational solidarity and loyalty.

2. The "Society" Versus the "Convention" Method

Even in the foreign mission organization, the Triennial Convention, tensions developed which hastened the separation of Baptists in the South from Baptists in the North. A debate continued for years between those who wished the Triennial Convention to become a real American Baptist convention for directing all the major activities of the denomination, and those who wished it to remain what it was. The latter group prevailed, primarily because of New England leadership, which was closer in larger numbers to the several societies, all located in Philadelphia, New York, and Boston, and the former group, largely in the South, much farther away.

3. Complaints Against the American Baptist Home Mission Society

The motto of the American Baptist Home Mission Society was "America for Christ." Baptists in the South and what was then the West soon began to complain that the society was not giving enough attention to their sections of the country. Many Southerners began to clamor for an organization that would do more to meet their needs.

The Society was aware of those needs. It made unsuccessful efforts to find qualified men who would go as missionaries to the South. It showed its sincerity by offering, 1834, to pay a missionary a hundred dollars a month instead of the usual hundred dollars a year if he would go to New Orleans. However, it failed to find a man who would go.

4. *The Primary Problem of Slavery*

Although there were other causes that led the South to separate from the Triennial Convention and the Home Mission Society, the principal cause was slavery. Of course, ultimately the question was far greater than the simple question of whether slave owners would be appointed as missionaries. In the answer to that question, the South saw wrapped up its whole distinctive culture and way of life. Slavery related to every facet of Southern existence. The South's economy was based upon slave labor, and the whole structure of Southern society was involved. Personal relations, the family, education, the arts, literature, recreation, and every other area of life was in some way affected by the existence of a large body of slaves in the South. It was manifestly impossible for the churches to be unaffected.

Christian leaders in the South expressed concern for the spiritual condition of the slaves and often urged that more be done for their religious life. Negroes were usually members of their masters' churches. Many attended regularly and participated in the worship. In some churches, there were galleries for the slaves, and Negro deacons to serve their race. Occasionally, Negroes were licensed to preach and given permission by their masters to preach to slaves not in their own church.

Although many Southerners accepted their responsibility to evangelize the slaves and provide church life for them, they vigorously opposed all measures taken to free the slaves, for their freedom threatened the way of life which the South knew. Therefore, when abolitionist Baptists in the North became more and more aggressive, most Baptists in the South became deeply concerned. By 1835, two-thirds of the delegates to the meeting of the New England Anti-Slavery Society were Baptist and Methodist ministers. The English Baptists, by resolution, frequently asked American Baptists to assume leadership in the antislavery movement.

5. *The Crisis*

Most American Baptist leaders, seeing the seed of disunion in the slavery issue, tried to neutralize the danger by insisting that their societies had no authority to involve themselves with reference to slavery. However, it became increasingly difficult to keep the issue from becoming dominant in the councils of the several Baptist societies after 1840, when a Baptist antislavery convention was formed, and a member of the board of the Triennial Convention, Elon Galusha, was elected as its president.

In both 1841 and 1844 the Triennial Convention (the foreign mission society) and the Home Mission Society definitely declared their neutrality on the slavery issue. The executive committee of the Georgia Baptist Convention asked the Home Mission Society to appoint J. E. Reeve, a Georgia slaveholder, as a missionary to the Indians, but it refused to do so. The Alabama Baptist Convention, in 1844, asked the acting board of the Triennial Convention if it would appoint a slaveholder as a foreign missionary. It replied that it would not. Thus it appeared to the Southerners that both boards had acted contrary to the policy their two societies had established.

The die was cast. Nearly all, both North and South, agreed that further co-operation between the two areas was impossible. Many deplored the necessity for separation, but few any longer believed it could be avoided.

II. The Convention Is Formed

1. The Virginia Baptist Foreign Mission Society Issues the Call

After the acting board of the Triennial Convention declared that it would not appoint a slaveholder as a missionary, a meeting of the whole board was called. Among those present were James B. Taylor and Jeremiah B. Jeter of Virginia, who were entertained by Francis Wayland. Even the moderate Wayland and his friends agreed that the separation of the Baptists, North and South, was best for all parties.

When Taylor and Jeter reported to the Virginia Baptist Foreign Mission Society, its board of managers issued a call for "a Convention to confer on the best means of promoting the Foreign Mission cause and other interests of the Baptists of the South."

2. The First Meeting of the Convention

Distances in the South were great, and many difficulties beset travelers, but the Baptists of the South responded heartily to the Virginia society's call and sent two hundred and ninety-three men to Augusta, Georgia, for a consultative convention. A total of three hundred and seventy-nine delegates had been elected by various

Baptist bodies, but fifty-two did not attend, and thirty-four represented two or more bodies. Of the eight states represented, Georgia had the most present, as would be expected. Next were South Carolina, Virginia, and Alabama. Maryland, North Carolina, and Louisiana had two persons present; and Kentucky and the Disrict of Columbia, one each. Mississippi, Arkansas, Florida, and Tennessee sent fraternal letters. The Convention met May 8, 1845, and elected William B. Johnson, of South Carolina, former president of the Triennial Convention, as its president.

3. *The Convention's Constitution*

After approving a preliminary report the Convention discussed a proposed constitution, and after some amendments it was unanimously adopted, including the name Southern Baptist Convention. Like the various Baptist societies of the North, it declared the United States to be its field. To emphasize its agreement with the original purpose of the Triennial Convention, it adopted word for word that convention's preamble as adopted in 1814, including the following, which was almost certainly written originally by President Johnson: "for the purpose of carrying into effect the benevolent intentions of our constituents, by organizing a plan for eliciting, combining and directing the energies of the whole denomination in one sacred effort, for the propagation of the Gospel."

The Convention, by adopting this constitution, brought into being a truly denominational body of the type which Luther Rice and others who agreed with him had advocated. They had intended that the Triennial Convention should be such an organization instead of becoming no more than a society for promoting foreign missions.

To make sure that there would be no misunderstanding as to the purpose of the new convention, the constitution clearly stated the purpose of the convention to be as follows: "to promote Foreign and Domestic Missions, and other important objects connected with the Redeemer's kingdom, and to combine for this purpose, such portions of the Baptist denomination in the United States as may desire a general organization for Christian benevolence." It specified that the Convention should meet triennially to elect as many boards of managers as in its judgment would "be necessary for carrying out the benevolent objects it may determine to promote."

It is difficult to overestimate the significance of the decision of the Southern Baptist Convention to choose the kind of organization which would include all objects of the churches' concern and thus encourage denominational unity. It resolved that it would care for all the interests of the churches without in any way depriving them of their autonomy and freedom. This action resulted in a strong denominational spirit among Southern Baptists that has contributed to their remarkable growth and enabled them properly to relate and integrate their varied activities and interests.

Perhaps more than any other man, President Johnson was immediately responsible for the decision to adopt the plan of organization which emerged. In his presidential address to the South Carolina Baptist State Convention the week before the Southern Baptist Convention was organized, he proposed a constitution which abandoned the "society" method and would employ "separate and independent bodies [boards] for the prosecution of each object," and thereby result in a "judicious concentration." This meant one convention "embodying the whole Denomination, together with separate and distinct Boards, for each object of benevolent enterprise, located at different places, and all amenable to the Convention."

The Convention's constitution provided for an organization which had a "judicious concentration" but it also declared that the general organization would "fully respect the independence and equal rights of the churches."

In addition, it provided that the membership of the Convention should consist of those "who contribute funds or are delegated by religious bodies contributing funds." It further sought to prevent too great a concentration of authority by locating its mission boards in different sections of the country, the board for foreign missions at Richmond, Virginia, and the board for domestic missions at Marion, Alabama.

At first no other boards or agencies than these two were organized. The American Baptist Publication Society continued to serve the needs of the South for some years. Its representative was usually present at the meetings of the Southern Baptist Convention, biennial rather than triennial from 1846.

III. A New Era Begins

Before the Convention adjourned May 12, it elected officers to serve until 1846 the time for the first regular session at Richmond.

Anxious to assure the world that the fellowship of Baptists in America had not been broken by its organization, the Southern Baptist Convention included in its public statement as to the need for such a convention this statement: "Let not the extent of this disunion be exaggerated . . . . Northern and Southern Baptists are still brethren. They differ in no article of faith. They are guided by the same principles of Gospel order."

Before the Convention met at Richmond it secured a charter under the laws of Georgia, and its newly appointed boards began to function. The Domestic Board put missionaries in the field immediately. In August the Foreign Board appointed Samuel Clopton and George Pearcy as missionaries to China.

A new era had begun in the history of American Baptists. The able men who organized the Convention at Augusta knew that what they were doing would have far-reaching consequences, and that there would inevitably be an opportunity for the Baptists of the country to judge between the value and effectiveness of loosely knit societies, and a cohesive and centralized denomination.

SUGGESTED TOPICS FOR DISCUSSION

1. Discuss the strong and weak points of the "society" and the "convention" types of organization.
2. What actions, if any, could have prevented the separation of Baptists, North and South?
3. Discuss the nature of the new Southern Baptist Convention.

CHAPTER 4 OUTLINE

I. BOARD OF FOREIGN MISSIONS
1. The First Secretary and Early Missionaries
2. Problems of Policy and Method
3. Early Mission Stations
4. Abram M. Poindexter
5. Two Great Crises

II. BOARD OF DOMESTIC MISSIONS
1. The Overwhelming Needs
2. Facing Great Difficulties
3. Heroism of Missionaries
4. New Demands upon the Board
5. The Disruptive Force of War

III. PUBLICATIONS AND SUNDAY SCHOOLS
1. The Southern Baptist Publication Society
2. The Bible Board
3. The First Sunday School Board

IV. BEGINNINGS IN THEOLOGICAL EDUCATION
1. Difficulties Relating to a Central Seminary
2. Efforts to Establish a Seminary
3. The Southern Baptist Theological Seminary Established
4. The Interruption of the War

V. THEOLOGICAL CONTROVERSY
1. The Rise and Influence of Landmarkism
2. The Crucial Convention of 1859

4

Progress and Storm

1845-1865

THE FOUNDERS of the Southern Baptist Convention were enthusiastic about the new organization and dedicated to its progress. At the same time they faced their problems realistically and were well aware of the many difficulties to be overcome. The South was sparsely settled. Churches often found their members scattered over many miles of territory in a period when transportation was difficult. The Southern Baptist ministry was not as a whole well trained, and in many instances pastors were poorly paid and had to obtain most of their income from other labor. Most churches were not interested in missions. The Triennial Convention's board in Boston was so far away that its influence was relatively weak in the South. Unfortunately also, the churches were not trained to systematic liberality.

In its first annual report, the Board of Foreign Missions called attention to these problems and pointed out that since Southern Baptists were principally farmers, and had to be visited upon their farms or gathered together in their churches, it was difficult to diffuse information and marshal support quickly. Cities, towns, and even villages were far apart. The work of the board's agents was consequently slow and beset with hardships.

Since both boards had to begin without missionaries or stations, schools or printing presses, and without the experience necessary for effective work, it is easy to understand why some said that the first regular meeting of the Convention "would number its days, and furnish materials for its entire history." These discouraging factors were not sufficient, however, to keep the young convention from pursuing a course of expansion and progress.

The Convention's advance was not seriously interrupted until the great conflict began between North and South. When that came in 1861, retrenchment became necessary, and years passed before full recovery was made.

I. BOARD OF FOREIGN MISSIONS

1. *The First Secretary and Early Missionaries*

The Foreign Mission Board was fortunate in having a strong man, James Barnett Taylor, as its first corresponding secretary. He was pastor of the Second Baptist Church in Richmond, and able to devote part of his time to the task. He was already well acquainted with the problems of missionary endeavor, having been president of the Virginia Baptist Foreign Mission Society when it issued the call for a consultative convention at Augusta. A wise and consecrated man, he continued as secretary until his death in 1871.

Fortunately, there was no long controversy over the adjustment of claims relative to property or missionaries between the Triennial Convention and the Southern Convention. The Triennial Convention retained its property and assumed all the debts. The missionaries were free to choose the board with which they would work. If any wished to transfer to the Foreign Board at Richmond, they were at liberty to do so. John Lewis Shuck, Virginia, who went to China as a missionary for the Triennial Convention in 1835, transferred and became the Southern Baptist Convention's first foreign missionary. Samuel C. Clopton and George Pearcy, appointed in August, 1845, went to China in 1846. Issachar J. Roberts, from Tennessee, and a missionary in Canton, China, also became a worker for the Richmond Board in 1846. China, therefore, became the first Southern Baptist foreign mission field.

2. *Problems of Policy and Method*

The Convention, at its first regular session in 1846, found itself already grappling with major policy problems in reference to its foreign mission program. Richard Fuller led the Convention to limit the fields which it would enter so that its energies would not be divided and weakened. It also recognized the part that all Christians have in evangelizing the world, and declared that it would look with favor upon the establishment of mission stations which would include "pious and intelligent merchants and mechanics." It also realized that a native ministry ought to be cultivated. From the very first it recognized the need for theological instruction for native preachers.

The Foreign Mission Board realized from the beginning the necessity of informing the people of its work and needs and of developing plans for raising the necessary money to meet its responsibilities. Though there was no "cooperative program," the word "co-operation" appeared prominently in the board's first report of the committee on agencies.

Agents to go about raising money for both the Foreign and Domestic boards were appointed. They raised most of the funds for many years. Vigorous criticism of this method was made from time to time, but years passed before a better method was devised.

A periodical for the Foreign Mission Board was recommended by the Convention in 1845. The *Southern Baptist Missionary Journal* soon began publication. By 1849, *The Commission* was also being published. Since the Board of Domestic [Home] Missions had no journal, the *Southern Baptist Missionary Journal* helped promote the interests of the Domestic Board as well. In 1851 the Convention approved a monthly, *The Home and Foreign Journal,* to replace the *Missionary Journal.*

3. *Early Mission Stations*

Before civil strife brought foreign missions among Southern Baptists to a temporary halt, the China mission was constantly being strengthened. Stations were maintained in Canton and Shanghai, and others were established. More than one hundred converts were baptized. In Africa, two missions were established, the Yoruba and the Liberian. Two other missions were attempted, though unsuccessfully. Thomas J. Bowen, Georgia, went to Yoruba as a missionary in 1849. His health failed, and he returned to the United States. In 1859 the Board sent him to Brazil to establish a mission, but it had to be abandoned in 1861 when his health completely failed.

Six years after the United States opened Japan to western influence, J. Q. L. Rohrer, Maryland, and his wife sailed from New York (August 3, 1860) to be the first Southern Baptist missionaries to that land. Unfortunately, they perished at sea. C. H. Toy, J. L. Johnson and his wife were also appointed, but did not go because of the Civil War.

4. Abram M. Poindexter

To assist Secretary Taylor in his increasingly heavy work, the Board, 1854, chose Rev. Abram M. Poindexter as his associate. A great orator, an impassioned preacher, and an able executive, he edited the magazine and did much field work. He helped to guide the denomination in the stormy and trying days before, during, and immediately after the Civil War.

5. Two Great Crises

The Foreign Mission Board faced two great crises in the latter part of the period under consideration. After 1858 it was for a number of years subjected to criticism and close scrutiny as a result of the Landmark controversy, about which more is said at another place in this book. The second great crisis was the war which broke out between the North and the South. This proved to be a major test. As early as 1861, the Foreign Mission Board reported that receipts had fallen off greatly, and that, almost certainly, it would not be able to meet its current liabilities. It had therefore to curtail its activities. The Federal blockade made communication with its missionaries in China and Africa nearly impossible. Though some funds were sent (under a flag of truce) to the board's financial agent in New York, the main support of the missionaries came from Maryland, the District of Columbia, Kentucky, and Missouri through the war period. A provisional board in Baltimore kept the work from having to be abandoned completely. Other expedients by which funds for the missionaries became available were the investment of the board in long-staple cotton to be run through the blockade and sold at high prices in England, the gifts of foreign residents in Shanghai and Canton and of the London Missionary Society, and finally, the undertaking of secular work by some of the missionaries. All these means enabled the board to emerge from the war with a debt of only $8,000, which was paid within three years.

II. Board of Domestic Missions

1. *The Overwhelming Needs*

As great as the need for foreign missions appeared to be, the task at home seemed no less challenging. In the fourteen states that the Board of Domestic Missions regarded as its territory, there were about eight million people scattered in an area of just over 950,000 square miles. To serve this tremendous area and these great numbers, Baptists had "about 2,000 preachers including the superannuated, and those of feeble and broken constitutions, together with those employed as teachers, farmers, merchants, mechanics, lawyers, &c." Even these few preachers were unequally distributed through the area. Many of the people, even of mature age, in every state had never heard the gospel. Though the needs of the white population were great, the board recognized that the needs of the Negroes were even greater. The major area of need was the Mississippi Valley, Florida, and Texas. The board also saw a special opportunity for ministering to the Mexicans in Texas near the border.

2. Facing Great Difficulties

In spite of the great needs which confronted Southern Baptists, it was difficult at first to secure proper support for the Board of Domestic Missions. In its first year it faced several crises. Its president, Basil Manly, Sr., resigned. J. B. Reynolds, the corresponding secretary, resigned soon after the Convention adjourned. His successor, D. P. Bestor, labored until November and then resigned. The treasurer also resigned. The Board's activities were almost paralyzed for a time. The problem all faced was summarized by Bestor: "I have learned by visiting many, and by extensive correspondence, that our brethren prefer carrying on their domestic missionary operations, through their Associations and State Conventions. They approve, invariably, of our Southern organization; but I cannot persuade them to act efficiently in its support."

A widespread criticism of the Board was its having agents in the field to publicize its activities and raise funds. As was true also with the Foreign Mission Board, agents were absolutely necessary if any funds at all were to be raised among the churches. Yet both boards had constantly to justify their use.

In spite, however, of all the difficulties, when the Convention met in 1846 the Board had six missionaries in service, and most of the state conventions had become auxiliaries to it.

3. *Heroism of Missionaries*

Whatever the difficulties of the Board were, the problems and heroism of the missionaries themselves should never be overlooked. One rather typical report came from missionary John Tucker, in Florida. He wrote:

"I am in a vast field of labor, having formed a circuit of about 450 miles in extent; and not an ordained preacher, but myself, in the whole bounds. Since the first of March last, I have received no support (only about $40, from the brethren and friends on the circuit). Since that time, I have travelled about 1,300 miles; visited and prayed with about 80 families; received and baptized about 20 on profession of their faith in Christ; have had four new meeting-houses finished, in as many settlements.

"In August, I had the help of Brother Daniel Edwards of Georgia about three weeks. We constituted five churches, ordained five deacons, and baptized four persons. There are now in the bounds of my circuit, six constituted churches. In several other settlements I have collected members and formed them into societies, preparatory to church organization, when I shall get help. I have about twenty settlements in which I preach. In some I hold two days' meetings. It takes about thirty days to go round my circuit, requiring more than half my time, as I perform the journey every two months. I have several Sabbath schools, and successfully inculcate the principles of temperance. I believe there is sound faith and correct practice among the brethren."

4. New Demands upon the Board

Though as early as 1849 there were demands that the Board of Domestic Missions enter into work in New Mexico and California, it declined, maintaining that it was best to confine its labors to the "Southern or slave-holding States." There was continued pressure upon it to enter the work in California. A demand to evangelize the Chinese there required consideration. There was some question whether labor among the Chinese belonged to the Domestic Board or the Foreign Board. It was decided that the locality of the field, not the character of the population, was the determining factor. The principle was laid down that all portions of the country were within the province of the Board of Domestic Missions. J. L. Shuck, who had been a missionary for the Foreign Board in China, resigned to become the Domestic Board missionary to the Chinese in California. In 1855 the Board reported that it had begun work among the Chinese and the Americans also.

The Board seemed to be rapidly accepting new responsibilities. A sharp debate in the Convention of 1855 centered around accepting the proffered transfer of the American Indian Mission Association to the Convention. The transfer was accepted, and the Board's name was changed to the Board of Domestic and Indian Missions. A resolution was also adopted calling upon the board to "occupy Kansas as soon as practicable [sic]." It did so in March, 1857. This early interest in the West revealed that people from the South were migrating westward. Few families were unaffected by this movement.

The Board also had to face the problems that arose in areas where Roman Catholics were dominant or strong. Its annual reports often referred to this problem. It took action in 1854 by establishing the Coliseum Baptist Church in New Orleans so that the denomination could have a point from which to work in the southern stronghold of Catholicism.

5. *The Disruptive Force of War*

The Civil War played havoc with the work of the Domestic Mission Board. Except for labor among the soldiers, it suspended almost all its work before the war ended. For example, only one missionary was among the Indians in 1863.

The chaplains, missionaries, and colporteurs did a remarkable work among the soldiers, as did similar workers of other denominations. Such generals as Robert E. Lee, Stonewall Jackson, and John B. Gordon encouraged it.

III. PUBLICATIONS AND SUNDAY SCHOOLS

The constitution of the Southern Baptist Convention stated that its purpose was to promote missions and "other important objects connected with the Redeemer's kingdom." It provided that as many boards of managers as might be necessary should be appointed.

Only two boards, one for foreign missions and one for domestic (home) missions, were established at first. At the Richmond convention, 1846, two additional boards were proposed. They were to take over the work in the South being done by the American Bible Society and the American and Foreign Bible Society, and the American Baptist Publication Society. After discussion the Convention asked its two boards to act as agents for the Bible societies in Bible distribution. The Convention decided that it would not be wise "to embarrass itself with any enterprise for the publication and sale of books."

1. The Southern Baptist Publication Society

May 13, 1847, at the annual session of the Georgia Baptist Convention, Savannah, Baptists from four states met and organized the Southern Baptist Publication Society, adopted a constitution, and located the society at Charleston, South Carolina, then the foremost publication center in the South. It was independent of the Southern Baptist Convention, and organized along the same lines as the various Baptist societies in the North. However, it and the Convention cordially co-operated. The Convention adjourned at a specified time for all to attend a meeting of the society when it met simultaneously with the Convention. The society's purpose was "to publish and distribute such books as are needed by the Baptist denomination in the South." It procured a charter from South Carolina in 1847, and opened its depository in February, 1848. In time, it had its own press.

The Southern Baptist Publication Society published helpful tracts and more than eighty books and booklets by Southern Baptist authors. The agencies in the South that had been auxiliary to the American Baptist Publication Society became auxiliary to it.

The Society also planned to print Sunday school books and helps as rapidly as its means would permit, but never did so.

From time to time members of both the Society and the Convention advocated its becoming a board of the Convention, but there was never enough support for it to be done. As time went on the society became involved in debt. It became a casualty of the Civil War in 1864.

2. *The Bible Board*

In May, 1851, the Southern Baptist Convention established a Bible board, and located it at Nashville, Tennessee. It had four secretaries by January, 1860, and was constantly handicapped by a lack of funds. Many Southern Baptists, instead of supporting it, made their gifts either to the American Bible Society (interdenominational) or the American and Foreign Bible Society of the Baptists of the North. Another society of the North, the American Bible Union, organized in 1850 chiefly by Baptists, increased the difficulties of the Bible Board.

During the secretaryship of Amos Cooper Dayton, 1854–1858, the Bible Board became deeply involved in the Landmark controversy. He was one of the three leaders of Landmarkism, the other two being James Robinson Graves and James Madison Pendleton. Opposition to Dayton became so strong that he resigned in April, 1858. At the Southern Baptist Convention, 1859, the Bible Board's first secretary, William C. Buck, strongly supported by Graves, moved to abolish the Bible Board, but the motion was lost.

At the 1861 session of the Convention, a committee was appointed to make a report in 1863 with reference to the consolidation of the Bible Board and the Southern Baptist Publication Society. After Nashville fell to the Union Army in February, 1862, the Bible Board ceased to operate. The Convention, 1863, not having definite information about it, abolished it. Less than a year thereafter, the Publication Society came to an end.

3. *The First Sunday School Board*

Though 1863 marked the end of the Bible Board, that did not mean that Southern Baptists had no interest in such matters as publications and Sunday schools. At the same convention which abolished the Bible Board a young professor in the recently created Southern Baptist Theological Seminary, Basil Manly, Jr., began to take a role in such matters. Manly's father, Basil Manly, Sr., had been a leading figure among Southern Baptists, and now his son began to loom as a prominent figure. Young Manly was particularly anxious for the Convention to do something about the promotion of Sunday schools and the distribution of Bibles and other religious publications. As a result of his magnificent appeal to the Convention, a Sunday School Board was created in 1863 in the very midst of war. He argued that though the American Sunday School Union was doing a fine work, it could not be as interested in instituting a Sunday school in every Baptist church as Southern Baptists themselves would be. He declared that the Convention could not wait until the end of the war, for the task was too important. Children were growing up without a knowledge of the

Bible, and Baptists had a compelling responsibility to them.

The Convention elected Manly president of the new board and located it at Greenville, South Carolina, where the seminary was. Another brilliant young professor of the seminary, John A. Broadus, served part time as corresponding secretary. Though the determination to employ a general Sunday school missionary for each state was only partly successful, several men of outstanding stature did serve. By 1865, several Sunday school helps were published. The most successful publication was begun in 1866, *Kind Words for the Sunday School Children.* It had a long and useful career.

With the South prostrate after the war, South Carolina particularly so, the Convention in 1868, after prolonged debate, transferred the Sunday School Board to Memphis, Tennessee. The Landmark controversy was still disturbing the Convention, and many feared that the Sunday School Board would be completely under Landmark influence, for Tennessee and Mississippi were Landmark strongholds. Thus much of the support the Board received at Greenville was lost. Funds were lacking for effective work. These difficulties were heightened by the great depression which began with Black Friday, September 24, 1869, culminating in the panic of 1873. Consequently, in May, 1873, the Convention merged the Sunday School Board with the Domestic and Indian Mission Board so that for a year there was the clumsily named Domestic and Indian Mission and Sunday School Board. This long name was changed to Home Mission Board in 1874.

Southern Baptists were in the midst of one of the

most discouraging periods of their history, and not until 1891 when recovery was being achieved would there be another independent board to promote Sunday school work.

IV. Beginnings in Theological Education

1. *Difficulties Relating to a Central Seminary*

When the Southern Baptist Convention was organized in Augusta in 1845, the question of a general theological seminary to serve all the Baptists of the South was not discussed in the sessions. However, there were those present who did raise the question privately, but found opposition to be formidable. At least two major roadblocks stood in the way of any central theological seminary. First, there was as yet no general agreement that ministers should be trained in such an institution. Not only was the general educational level in the Southern Baptist ministry low, but there were strong men who believed that a college was the place to train ministers. Several states had colleges of their own in which the theological department was prominent. They saw no need for a seminary. The Western Baptist Theological Institute began at Covington, Kentucky, in 1845, but numerous difficulties soon led to its discontinuance.

2. *Efforts to Establish a Seminary*

In spite of opposition, the advocates of a Baptist seminary to serve the whole of the South increased in strength, and several conferences were held from 1847 and after to consider the problem. R. B. C. Howell,

Nashville, was the principal leader of these early efforts.

The Convention did not involve itself in these plans for a central theological seminary. Rather, its advocates usually met at some convenient time preceding or after the convention sessions. They took specific actions regarding the organization of a seminary at Augusta, Georgia, 1856, and Louisville, Kentucky, 1857. The names of Manly, Poindexter, Jeter, and Boyce appear prominently in the proceedings of these conferences. The Louisville conference accepted an offer from the South Carolina Convention to turn the theological fund of Furman University over to the trustees of the new school, and voted to increase the fund to $100,000. The conditions attached were that the seminary should be located at Greenville, South Carolina, and that the other states should raise a like amount of money.

3. *The Southern Baptist Theological Seminary Established*

As the result of Furman University's action, a convention assembled, May 1, 1858, at Greenville to establish a general theological seminary. With Basil Manly, Sr., serving as president, the convention adopted a plan of organization which included the "legal and practical arrangements" drawn up by Boyce, the "abstract of doctrines and principles" written by Manly, and the "plan of instruction" which Broadus had modeled after the University of Virginia elective system. The plan of organization incorporated the ideas of James Boyce. They have been fundamental in the organization of each of the Southern Baptist theological seminaries. Summarily stated, they proposed (1) that the seminary should admit men not only of college education, but those who had been kept from obtaining more than "a common English education"; (2) that the seminary should offer such courses as would enable the best students to receive an education equivalent to that anywhere obtainable; and (3) that each professor should be required upon inauguration to sign an abstract of principles.

The Seminary was not at first owned by the Southern Baptist Convention, but its charter called for the trustees to be members of regular Baptist churches. The Southern Baptist Convention nominated three men for each vacancy on the board of trustees, though the board itself was self-perpetuating. The internal government of the seminary was put in the hands of the faculty who were regarded as equal in position, but were presided over by a chairman appointed by the board.

The Seminary began its first session in the fall of 1859 with its four young professors full of enthusiasm and well qualified for their positions. Twenty-six students enrolled for the first session, more than had attended the first session of any other theological school in America.

4. *The Interruption of the War*

Unfortunately, the coming of war changed the rosy prospects. After its third session the Seminary suspended operations until after the war because no exemptions from military service were given to ministerial students.

When the Seminary reopened in November, 1865, with only seven students, it faced almost insurmountable difficulties. The four professors covenanted, in response to Broadus's appeal, that though the seminary might die they would die first. Dr. Broadus had only one student (he was blind) in his course on preaching, but he so carefully prepared his lectures that from them came his famous book, *The Preparation and Delivery of Sermons*. It is still widely used.

V. THEOLOGICAL CONTROVERSY

1. *The Rise and Influence of Landmarkism*

In 1854, James R. Graves printed an essay by James M. Pendleton, "Ought Baptists to recognize Pedobaptist preachers as gospel ministers?" and gave it the title, "An Old Landmark Reset." (Pendleton's answer to his question was no.) In the controversies that followed, the term "Landmarkism" was used to designate the doctrinal views of Graves and his associates and adherents.

The Landmark doctrine was first stated at the session of the Big Hatchie Association, 1851, at Cotton Grove near Memphis, Tennessee. Graves immediately became the leader of Landmarkism, and for many years kept Southern Baptists in turmoil because of its doctrines and their relationship to denominational life.

The substance of the Cotton Grove affirmations was that other churches such as Methodist, Presbyterian, and Episcopalian, all others but Baptist, were not churches, but societies; their ministers should not be recognized as gospel ministers or permitted to preach in Baptist pulpits; and members of all such churches should not be called "brethren."

Four years later (1855) a heated debate occurred in the Southern Baptist Convention concerning its recognition of ministers of other denominations. Until then the convention practice had been to invite ministers present from other denominations to participate in its deliberations. The Landmarkers challenged this practice, not only then but later. The controversy rose to fever pitch throughout the convention territory. The Baptist papers gave much space to it.

Other Landmark doctrines appeared and were debated. These included (1) the claim that Baptist churches possessed an unbroken succession from the first church in Jerusalem; (2) the conviction that there is no valid meaning to the word "church" apart from the local church, and that the kingdom is the sum total of all local churches; (3) opposition to alien immersion (not held exclusively by them); and (4) that the Lord's Supper was to be observed by one only in the church where he had his membership.

The Landmark doctrine that most endangered the Southern Baptist Convention was that its "missionary machinery" was unscriptural. Graves and his associates charged that the two mission boards had no right to examine, appoint, and direct missionaries, or to pay their salaries. They maintained that the churches should appoint their own missionaries; that the missionaries should do their work in their own way; and that the boards should do no more than transmit the funds that the churches sent to them.

2. The Crucial Convention of 1859

The Landmarkers were aggressive, determined, and

persistent. They gained control of the Bible Board for several years. In 1859, at the Richmond session of the Convention, they tried to take from its boards the right to select and direct the missionaries. A tense debate of more than a day developed. The delegates voted overwhelmingly in favor of the convention's methods through its two boards, but directed the Foreign Board to transmit funds churches might send it for their missionaries.

Landmarkers established a publication house, and, in 1859, the Southern Baptist Sunday School Union. These were largely to promote the Landmark cause. The doctrinal controversies became involved in personal conflicts, and, at times, imperiled organized work in associations and state conventions in addition to the Southern Baptist Convention. The Graves-Howell controversy, (1857–1862), for example, had its origin largely in Landmarkism.

Landmarkers threatened to divide the Convention at Richmond in 1859, and imperiled Baptist organized life all over the South.

By February, 1862, when the Union army captured Nashville, Landmark headquarters, the tide had already turned against the Landmarkers, and division had been avoided. However, the controversy simmered for some years, and then broke out anew concerning "Gospel Missionism." Beyond doubt, the prolonged controversy profoundly influenced the total life of Southern Baptists, both in doctrines and methods. The denomination's attitude towards other religious bodies through the years has been largely due to Landmark emphases and beliefs.

SUGGESTED TOPICS FOR DISCUSSION

1. To what extent are the problems which the boards of Foreign Missions and Domestic Missions faced in their first years still problems today?
2. To what extent are the three ideas of Boyce relating to theological education relevant today?
3. Discuss the effect of war upon religious life giving special attention to the effect of the Civil War upon the Southern Baptist Convention.

CHAPTER 5 OUTLINE

I. FOREIGN MISSIONS
  1. New Fields Entered
  2. Strong Leadership

II. THE BOARD OF DOMESTIC MISSIONS AND ITS STRUGGLE FOR SURVIVAL
  1. Competing Agencies Threaten Its Existence
  2. The Crisis Is Met
  3. Controversy with American Baptist Home Mission Society
  4. Board Prospers Under Tichenor

III. SOUTHERN BAPTIST THEOLOGICAL SEMINARY
  1. Lean Days
  2. Removal to Louisville
  3. Securing the Seminary's Position

IV. GROWING PAINS
  1. The Passing of the "Fathers"
  2. Annual Sessions
  3. P. H. Mell and Parliamentary Order
  4. Constitutional and Organizational Problems
  5. Religious Liberty
  6. A Bright Future

5

Painful Recovery

1866-1890

THE DESTRUCTIVE WAR was over, but the suffering and privations of the South were far from complete. In fact, in some respects the poverty and distress that prevailed immediately after the war, combined with the repressive policies of Reconstruction, were harder to bear than the war itself. Desolation was king! As W. H. Whitsitt put it a few years later, "Almost everything was destroyed except the courage of the people."

Many church buildings had been destroyed by the violence of the conflict or had been dismantled through military occupation. The work of the Southern Baptist Convention, which had been greatly impeded by the war, now faced the imminent peril of failing altogether in the face of the distressing conditions which prevailed. There was almost nothing to encourage the South. Money was very scarce, the people were dispirited, there was an uncertain state of affairs, both politically and commercially, and things generally were paralyzed. It is no wonder, then, that the Convention in 1867 recommended "a day of fasting, humiliation, and prayer, on account of the distressed condition of the country."

So far as the Southern Baptist Convention was concerned, 1879 proved to be a year of crisis, for it had to decide whether or not it would gird itself and go forward or completely abandon its high goals. It decided to press onward, and made remarkable progress. By the end of the period which this chapter considers it was once more well established and prosperous.

I. FOREIGN MISSIONS

1. *New Fields Entered*

Because of gifts during the war from churches in Maryland, District of Columbia, and Kentucky, and the willingness of the missionaries to engage in self-supporting labors, the Foreign Mission Board emerged from the war with a debt of only $8,000. Though any indebtedness constituted a major problem, the Foreign Mission Board was in a more favorable position than either of the other boards of the Convention. Though its struggle for survival was real, the board never had any intention of giving up or retrenching any more than was absolutely necessary. In fact, the opposite was the case, for in 1870 the board entered a new field. W. N. Cote became the convention's first missionary in Italy. Though the work in Italy was not without its difficulties and troubles, it was put on a solid foundation in 1873 by the arrival of George B. Taylor, a son of the board's secretary, James B. Taylor.

In this period also the Brazilian mission, abandoned in 1860, was again established. Work began in 1879 through a little church composed of Southerners who migrated to Brazil at the close of the Civil War, and was reinforced in 1881 by the arrival of Mr. and Mrs. W. B. Bagby. By 1898 the Brazilian work was well established, and a period of remarkable progress was at hand.

One of the most fruitful and progressive missions begun in this period was that in Mexico. It, too, was begun by a group of Southerners who migrated into Mexico. Though a Baptist church was organized in 1864, it was not until 1882 that missionaries under the appointment of the Foreign Mission Board were actually on Mexican soil.

In 1889, the Board opened work in Japan, and thereby fulfilled a desire which it expressed before the Civil War.

2. Strong Leadership

Thus, in foreign missions, Southern Baptists had a will to go on in spite of all the difficulties. Through this period, too, they were fortunate to have strong leadership in the Foreign Mission Board. Dr. Taylor continued to serve as secretary until 1872. His successor, Rev. Henry Allen Tupper, Sr., served from 1872 till 1893. In 1890, 78 missionaries and 86 native assistants were serving in the several mission fields of the Southern Baptist Convention. During that year the Board received $109,174.

II. The Board of Domestic Missions and Its Struggle for Survival

The war and its aftermath, which took its toll of everything, nearly cost the life of the Board of Indian and Domestic Missions. When, as a result of the disorganization and spiritual destitution left in the wake of war and reconstruction, the Board was most needed, it could do but little. The impoverished South could not adequately support it. The outlook was dark indeed.

1. *Competing Agencies Threaten Its Existence*

The American Baptist Home Mission Society and the American Baptist Publication Society, possessing greater material resources, sought to aid the churches in the South. They were especially active in the states west of the Mississippi River, though the other southern states were not neglected. Several state conventions in the South allied themselves with the two societies. Though the motives of the Northern societies were above reproach, it was inevitable that this situation would further weaken the position of the Board of Indian and Domestic Missions.

The desperate situation in the South led to some discussion as to the wisdom of some sort of reunion between Southern and Northern Baptists.

Fraternal messengers from the American Baptist Home Mission Society attended the Southern Convention at Baltimore, 1868, and offered the suggestion that the denomination "should 'work together,' in relation to a common end, with enlargedness of heart, with harmony of aims, keeping the unity of the spirit and the bond of peace." Although the discussions continued several years, there seemed to be no widespread sentiment for reunion on the part of the South. The Convention, 1870, decided that both it "and its boards should be maintained in their integrity."

The critical situation of the Domestic Board grew worse before it improved. The American Baptist Home Mission Society became so strong in the South and the Domestic Mission Board was in such desperate straits that suggestions were made in 1871 that it should be merged into the Board of Foreign Missions. For several years thereafter debate continued as to the need for the Domestic Mission Board. Several state conventions tried to prevent the Domestic Board from collecting funds or doing missionary work in their areas. No wonder, then, that the Board's indebtedness increased until it almost equaled its annual income.

2. *The Crisis Is Met*

A major crisis was reached at the Convention session at Atlanta in 1879. It was precipitated by a resolution offered by Isaac T. Tichenor, then president of a state college at Auburn, Alabama. He proposed that a meeting of representatives from all parts of the country be held to propose plans of co-operation between the Convention and other Baptist bodies. Though he later declared that the resolutions were not intended in anywise to bring about the dissolution of the Convention, but rather to strengthen it by defining its territorial limits and by securing the co-operation of the Northern societies in this matter, some interpreted it otherwise and brought the issue of the continuance of the convention to a head. The dramatic situation helped to solidify sentiment throughout the South in support of the Southern agencies. John A. Broadus, president of the Southern Baptist Theological Seminary, realized that the life of the seminary was involved in the life of the convention. It finally adopted his resolution declaring that though a fraternal spirit should exist between Baptists in all parts of the country, separate organizations should be preserved with no thought of a single national organization. Since that day no serious question has been raised concerning the continuance of the Southern Baptist Convention.

The Convention, having now definitely determined to press forward, set about the reconstruction of the Home Mission Board. To do this it took two significant actions in 1882. First, it moved the board from Marion, Alabama, where it had been located since 1845, to rapidly developing Atlanta, Georgia. Second, it elected Isaac T. Tichenor, an able, aggressive, and experienced leader, as the board's secretary.

3. Controversy with American Baptist Home Mission Society

Increasing opposition to the activity of the American Baptist Home Mission Society in the South helped to perfect the renewed determination to maintain and strengthen the Southern Baptist Convention. A controversy concerning the right of the society to work in the South began in August, 1882, when E. T. Winkler, president of the Home Mission Board, wrote an article in which he declared that the society's action constituted "intrusion" and "invasion," and called upon the churches of the Southern Baptist Convention to support their own board.

The corresponding secretary of the American Baptist Home Mission Society, H. L. Morehouse, replied vigorously to Winkler. He said that the society was in the South to stay, and that it had the right to work wherever it chose. He called attention to the fact that from the beginning the society had been dedicated to the winning of North America to Christ, and had never been a party to drawing territorial lines. Furthermore, he said that the state conventions in the Southwest, where the principal controversy raged, had invited it to aid them.

4. *Board Prospers Under Tichenor*

In the meantime, the new corresponding secretary of the Home Mission Board was gaining the confidence of the denomination. As a result of his aggressive leadership, the board prospered and again became dominant in the South. All the state conventions in time became its hearty supporters. The convention idea was coming to maturity in the South, and a growing denominational consciousness developed among Southern Baptists. I. T. Tichenor was justly called the "father of co-operation."

III. SOUTHERN BAPTIST THEOLOGICAL SEMINARY

1. *Lean Days*

Against overwhelming odds, the four dedicated Seminary professors reopened it in 1865. Lean days followed, however, and Dr. Boyce had to exert himself to the utmost to keep the institution open. Once the professors received no salary for twelve months.

One can understand the distress and humiliation under which they worked during those years of trial. Though repeatedly invited to go elsewhere, they stood by the work which they felt the Lord had committed to them. When Dr. Boyce was urged to accept the presidency of the South Carolina Railroad Company at a yearly salary of $10,000, he said: "Thank these gentlemen for me, but tell them I must decline, as I have decided to devote my life, if need be, to building up the Southern Baptist Theological Seminary."

2. *Removal to Louisville*

It soon became clear that adequate financial support would compel the Seminary to move from the poverty-stricken Deep South. Efforts to move it began in 1869 when the trustees of Union University, Murfreesboro, Tennessee, invited the seminary to establish itself there. Other offers were made, but the one from Louisville, Kentucky, was the most attractive. The Southern Baptist Convention, 1873, heartily approved its removal. The seminary moved from Greenville to its new location in 1877.

3. *Securing the Seminary's Position*

Though the financial burdens at Louisville were somewhat lighter, they were, nevertheless, far from satisfactory. To give it security some large gifts for endowment were necessary. When a new crisis developed, Joseph E. Brown, a former Georgia governor, gave the Seminary $50,000. Other large contributions followed to guarantee the seminary's permanence.

As the graduates of the Seminary became prominent pastors and leaders in Southern Baptist work, its usefulness increased. Its president, Dr. Boyce, was president of the Southern Baptist Convention for the eight sessions 1872–1879, and again in 1888. By 1890, its enrolment reached 150.

IV. GROWING PAINS

1. *The Passing of the "Fathers"*

As time passed, the Southern Baptist Convention paid

tribute one by one to those who brought it to birth and who helped it to live and become strong. In 1868, for example, it paid memorial tribute to its first two presidents—William Bullein Johnson, president from 1845 through 1849, and Robert Boyte Crawford Howell, president from 1851 till 1859.

2. *Annual Sessions*

The Convention's growth made more frequent sessions necessary. Triennial sessions were held in 1846 and 1849; biennial sessions, from 1851 through 1867; and then annual sessions. (The session due in 1865 was not held because of chaotic conditions the last year of the Civil War. A called session met at Russellville, Kentucky, in 1866.)

3. *P. H. Mell and Parliamentary Order*

Parliamentary procedures varied in the Convention. Richard Fuller, president in 1859 and 1861, able and greatly beloved, was no parliamentarian. This may have partly caused the Convention in 1863 to choose for its next president Patrick Hues Mell, president of the University of Georgia, who became one of the great parliamentarians of all time. He presided so efficiently and fairly that the Convention re-elected him eight successive sessions, 1863–1871. Then after eight years of service by Dr. Boyce, 1872–1879, it again elected Mell for seven terms, 1880–1887. He served fifteen years, longer than any president in the Convention's history.

At the request of the Convention, 1867, Dr. Mell wrote *A Manual of Parliamentary Practice*. The Convention adopted it as its rules of order, 1868, and used it until it adopted Franklin Howard Kerfoot's *Parliamentary Law* in 1900.

4. *Constitutional and Organizational Problems*

Though Convention organization was simple in comparison with that of today, constitutional and organizational problems were nevertheless important. Article III, on the membership of the Convention, proved especially troublesome, as it has through much of the Convention's history. The question of inviting visiting brethren to seats in the Convention also continued to perplex the "delegates." The practice of inviting only visiting Baptist ministers became usual.

By 1870, the Convention, having become dissatisfied with the sketchy annual financial reports from its boards, requested them to give "a comprehensive view of all the pecuniary transactions of the boards."

5. *Religious Liberty*

The Convention became particularly exercised about interference in the work of the churches by civil and military authorities during the latter part of the Civil War and the period of reconstruction. It was as concerned about religious liberty as it was about its property and activities. More than once the convention reasserted the historic Baptist convictions regarding religious liberty.

6. *A Bright Future*

By 1890 the South and Southern Baptists had recovered sufficiently from the effects of the Civil War to be optimistic about the future. The Convention was facing a new day, and was conscious of it. The journey through war and reconstruction had been long and painful; but, by the grace of God, a new day was dawning!

SUGGESTED TOPICS FOR DISCUSSION

1. Discuss the effects of the reconstruction era on Southern Baptists.
2. Are any of the problems of this period still problems today? If so, name and discuss them.
3. What other agencies or institutions, not owned or controlled by the Convention, were making significant contributions to Southern Baptists?

I. MISSIONARY PROGRESS
   1. Foreign Mission Work
   2. Home Missions
   3. Woman's Missionary Union
   4. Layman's Missionary Movement

II. EDUCATIONAL WORK OF THE CONVENTION
   1. The Sunday School Board
   2. Baptists and Higher Education
      (1) The Education Board
      (2) Southern Baptist Theological Seminary
      (3) Southwestern Baptist Theological Seminary
      (4) The Baptist Bible Institute

III. THE CONVENTION AND SOCIAL CONCERN
   1. Care of the Sick
   2. Relief and Annuity Board
   3. Committee on Temperance and Social Service

IV. SOUTHERN BAPTISTS AND THE CHRISTIAN WORLD
   1. The Baptist World Alliance
   2. Interdenominational Co-operation

6

Striding Ahead

1891-1919

WE COME NOW in our Baptist story to the beginning of the period in Southern Baptist life when events moved so rapidly that we can do little more than paint our picture with broad strokes, leaving for others the fascinating details.

How rapidly the Southern Baptist Convention developed is illustrated by the fact that while the proceedings of the 1890 Convention listed only the officers of the Convention and the members of two mission boards, the proceedings for 1919, almost three decades later, listed three additional boards: the Sunday School Board, the Relief and Annuity Board, and the Education Board. It also listed the Executive Committee, the Layman's Missionary Movement, the board of directors of New Orleans Baptist Bible Institute, the Committee on Temperance and Social Service, the Sunday School Lesson Committee, the Committee on International Baptist Memorial, and the officers of the Woman's Missionary Union, auxiliary to the Convention. Both conventions heartily approved and supported the work of the Southern Baptist Theological Seminary.

Attendance on the sessions of the Convention increased more than fourfold during the period under consideration: 801 were present in 1890, and 4,250 in

1919. Three additional states were represented at the Convention in 1919: Illinois, New Mexico, and Oklahoma. The membership of the Convention more than doubled in the twenty-nine years, increasing from 1,235,765 in 1890 to 2,961,348 in 1919. The total contributions of the churches for all causes increased from $2,876,927 in 1890 to $21,327,446 in 1919. Contributions to missions made an equally significant advance.

I. MISSIONARY PROGRESS

1. *Foreign Mission Work*

Foreign mission work advanced under the leadership of Robert J. Willingham, secretary from 1893 to 1914. Like his predecessor Henry Allen Tupper, who served from 1872 to 1893, Dr. Willingham gave himself unstintingly to the cause to which he was devoted. Contributions to foreign missions increased from $154,686 in 1893 to $691,500 in 1914, missionaries increased from 92 to 300, and members of mission churches grew from 2,923 to 30,000. James F. Love succeeded Dr. Willingham as secretary of the Board as the period drew toward a close.

The Board carefully cultivated the fields where it was working and judiciously opened others. In China, where the board began its work, many significant advances were made. Among these were the opening of work in interior China, the founding of Shanghai College in cooperation with Northern Baptists, the beginning of medical missions, the organization of the China Baptist Publication Society, and the general expansion of evangelistic and educational work.

Though the Liberian mission was closed in 1875, the Board greatly strengthened its mission program in Nigeria during this period. Medical work was begun in 1906; several schools, including one for girls, were organized; and the foundations for a seminary were laid. The story of missions is replete with heroic deeds, but nowhere did it take more courage and dedication for missionaries than in Africa. Many suffered, and some died from Malaria, yellow fever, and other diseases.

Some of the most remarkable advances occurred in Latin America, where Baptists had just established small mission stations at the time the period opened. By 1919 there was an exceptionally strong work in Brazil and significant work also in Argentina, Chile, and Mexico.

Work, which had just begun in Japan, grew steadily. By 1919, twenty missionaries were there, and educational and publication work had been inaugurated.

In Europe, Southern Baptist work was confined almost entirely to Italy. The work there was slow, but not without encouragement. The Whittinghills and the Everett Gills especially did significant work.

With the close of World War I and a great upsurge of interest in missions, an appeal for further expansion was made. The Layman's Missionary Movement, organized in 1907, served to underline the need. As a result, the Convention adopted a program to raise $75,000,000 in five years (1919–1924) for all its missionary work. This revealed the tremendous enthusiasm and optimism which pervaded the Convention.

The only major discordant note relative to foreign missions during this period was the continuing Landmark controversy as Gospel Missionism. Essentially, it rejected the methods employed by the mission boards and desired instead that the churches themselves should choose, direct, and support their own missionaries. T. P. Crawford and several other missionaries to China so agitated for their point of view that they either resigned or were asked by the Foreign Mission Board to sever their connection with it. The Southern Baptist Convention overwhelmingly sustained the Foreign Mission Board in this matter. The Landmark churches and associations, especially in Texas and Arkansas, then organized the Baptist General Association with Texarkana, Arkansas-Texas, as their headquarters, and established there a publication house and a book store. They changed their name, 1924, to the American Baptist Association. In 1950, when a split occurred, the minority withdrew and organized the North American Baptist Association, with headquarters at Little Rock, Arkansas. Both groups, however, continued their Landmark principles, including direct missions by the churches.

2. Home Missions

The energetic policy which Dr. Tichenor began during the previous period was continued after his retirement in 1899 by his successors: F. H. Kerfoot, F. C. McConnell, and B. D. Gray. This period was characterized by the establishment of a system of mountain schools, the strengthening of rural work, the extension of frontier missions, the establishment of a church building loan fund, the development of co-operative work among the Negroes, and several growing pains.

The growing pains were essentially twofold: first, the

development of a measure of friction between some of the state conventions and the Southern Baptist Convention; and second, the tensions involved in the relation between the American Baptist Home Mission Society and the Home Mission Board.

In regard to the first, state convention lines were more carefully drawn. Previously, for various reasons two or more general bodies existed in one state, or a general body might include territory in more than one state. Tichenor urged the unification of the general bodies along state lines. This strengthened state work. As long as the state boards and the boards of the Southern Baptist Convention agreed, all was well. When, at times, their interests clashed, some friction occurred.

These increasing problems of co-operation and co-ordination which came with the rapid increase in the size and the work of the Convention led to the appointment of a centennial committee. It made recommendations in 1900 that led to the establishment of a committee on co-operation. Though this committee did not itself become a powerful co-ordinating agency, its existence reflected the growing conviction that some such agency was necessary. It led to the creation of the Executive Committee in 1917 "to act for the body between its sessions" in ways which were defined.

The second principal growing pain came from the relations between the Home Mission Board and the American Baptist Home Mission Society. Secretary Tichenor, who charged that the society was "invading" the South, was anxious to arrive at an understanding with it about territorial limits.

In 1894, committees from the Southern Convention

and one from the Society met at Fortress Monroe, Virginia, and reached an amicable agreement as to the work among the Negroes and the question of territorial limits. As to the agreement regarding territory they said:

"We believe that . . . it is inexpedient for two different organizations of Baptists to solicit contributions or to establish missions in the same locality, and for this reason we recommend to the Home Mission Board of the Southern Baptist Convention and to the American Baptist Home Mission Society that, in the prosecution of their work already begun on contiguous fields or on the same field, all antagonisms be avoided and that their officers and employees be instructed to co-operate in all practicable ways in the spirit of Christ. That we further recommend to these bodies and their agents, in opening new work, to direct their efforts to localities not already occupied by the other."

About 1907, churches in New Mexico, which was in Society territory, began repeatedly to request assistance from the Home Mission Board. This led to friction with the newly formed Northern Baptist Convention. A conference between the parties involved was held at Washington, D.C., in 1909. All agreed that the Fortress Monroe agreement of 1894 had expired, and that its provisions were no longer in force. The Convention, when it adopted the Washington agreement, asserted the right of every church to determine its own alignment and co-operation.

Because the Home Mission Society was unhappy about the situation, new conferences were held, first at Old Point Comfort, Virginia, in 1911, and later at Hot

Springs, Arkansas, in 1912. The results were the adoption of a statement of principles by both conventions in 1912 which reasserted the independence of the local Baptist church, the moral interdependence and the cooperation of churches, and the advisory nature of denominational organizations. It was agreed that denominational organizations "should zealously regard the rights of all sister organizations, and of the church, being always careful to promote unity and harmony," and that "no Baptist body should use its influence to disintegrate or injure the work of any other Baptist bodies."

The principles of comity laid down in the agreement of 1912 have been repeatedly reaffirmed. Essentially, they represent the position of the Southern Baptist Convention today.

3. *Woman's Missionary Union*

Perhaps the most far-reaching development in terms of missions during the period 1891–1919 was the rapid growth of missionary interest among women and the remarkable development of the Woman's Missionary Union. Long before the WMU, local bands of women organized into little societies to raise funds for missionary work and other purposes. An interdenominational Woman's Union Missionary Society organized at Brooklyn, New York, 1860, inspired Mrs. Ann J. Graves, the mother of a missionary to China, to lead in the organization of the Woman's Mission to Woman at Baltimore, Maryland, in 1871.

The movement soon spread to other southern states. Dr. H. A. Tupper, the corresponding secretary of the Foreign Mission Board, gave it sympathetic support.

After 1871, the Convention minutes make frequent mention of the women's work. The Foreign Mission Board recommended that central committees be organized in each state to direct the work. Several were then formed, and in 1883 a separate woman's meeting was held during the Southern Baptist Convention.

Following the women's organizations, the question of whether or not a woman could properly be a member of the Convention became a live issue. On at least two earlier occasions a woman had been a member of the Convention, but by 1885 the issue had become so sharp that two women appointed by the Arkansas State Convention as its representatives were refused seats in the Convention. From that year until 1918, when women were admitted, only "brethren" were eligible for Convention membership. This made it impossible for the women to organize their work in any but an auxiliary relationship to the Convention. So representatives met at Richmond, Virginia, 1888, and organized the Woman's Missionary Union as an auxiliary to the Convention.

From the headquarters, first at Baltimore, came many important developments of Baptist missionary work. The Christmas offering suggested by Lottie Moon began in 1888. The graded system of missionary organization and education rapidly developed. Another far-reaching development was the assumption by the Woman's Missionary Union of the control of the Woman's Training School which, since 1904, had been operated by the Louisville Seminary.

4. Layman's Missionary Movement

An interdenominational gathering at New York in

1906 commemorated the centennial of the foreign mission movement in America. It so impressed a group of laymen that they established the Layman's Missionary Movement. Its purpose was to promote interest and participation in the missionary enterprise.

Like several other denominations, the Southern Baptist Convention soon responded to the appeal of the movement and gave it approval in 1907. The executive committee of the Layman's Missionary Movement among Southern Baptists elected John T. Henderson general secretary. He labored unceasingly and effectively to educate the laymen with regard to missions, and to organize and inspire them in its support. In 1926, this movement became the Baptist Brotherhood of the South.

II. Educational Work of the Convention

1. *The Sunday School Board*

In another place the story of the first Sunday School Board and its untimely end in 1873 has been told. Only its little periodical, *Kind Words,* survived. The Home Mission Board published it until 1891, and then turned it over to the second Sunday School Board at its organization. Its editor, Samuel Boykin, who served from the Memphis days of the first Sunday School Board in 1869 until his death in 1899, was the only human link between the two boards.

I. T. Tichenor, secretary of the Home Board, was anxious for Southern Baptists to publish their own Sunday school helps. Many leaders thought this was both unnecessary and unwise, for the Amercian Baptist Publication Society had many friends in the South and great resources.

In 1890, James M. Frost proposed, through an article in the *Religious Herald,* Virginia, the creation of a new board to have charge of publications and Sunday school interests. At the Convention that year Dr. Frost advocated a board of publication of the Southern Baptist Convention. The Convention was not yet ready for such a board, but it created a Sunday school committee and located it at Louisville, Kentucky.

At Birmingham, in 1891, the committee's first and only report to the Convention recommended the establishment of a Sunday school board. Dr. J. B. Gambrell, a highly respected minister, vigorously supported the American Baptist Publication Society and therefore opposed the formation of the board. He and Dr. Frost, the strong advocate of the board, were appointed as a subcommittee to formulate the report of the whole committee to which the recommendation for a Sunday school board had been referred. In a providential way their opposing views were reconciled. A Sunday school board, to be located in Nashville, Tennessee, was proposed. The Convention adopted the report without discussion, and with only thirteen dissenting votes.

Dr. Frost was chosen to be the Board's first secretary. He began work July, 1891, and served eighteen months. He then resigned to become pastor of the First Baptist Church, Nashville, and was elected president of the board. Theodore P. Bell, assistant corresponding secretary of the Foreign Mission Board, and a member of Dr. Frost's church at Richmond, from which he came to the Sunday School Board, succeeded him. In January,

1896, he and Isaac J. Van Ness bought the *Christian Index*, Atlanta, Georgia. He resigned his position with the board, and was succeeded by Dr. Frost, who then served until his death in October, 1916.

The American Baptist Publication Society proved to be a strong competitor of the new Sunday School Board, and even once proposed, in 1896, to absorb the board and its work. However, in spite of all difficulties, the board prospered from the first, and after 1897 its continued existence was assured beyond all doubt.

From the beginning, the Sunday School Board prepared a series of periodicals based on the International Uniform Lessons. Southern Baptists participated in the work of the lesson committee of the International Sunday School Association. However, they and some other denominations became dissatisfied with the way the affairs of the association were managed, and in 1910 the Sunday School Council of Evangelical Denominations was formed. Southern Baptists participated in this council during the rest of this period.

In addition to the lesson publishing phase of the Sunday School Board's work, the board began its history of book publishing in 1897 with the publication of Charles E. Taylor's *The Story of Yates the Missionary*.

At the turn of the century B. W. Spilman, of North Carolina, was employed as a field secretary to stir up the interest of the people in the improvement of Sunday schools. In 1903, the Board began the publication of some small volumes for teacher training, and the familiar study course books had thereby been set on their way.

The year in which the Sunday School Board was

established, 1891, the first national convention of the Baptist Young People's Union of America met at Chicago. The movement soon spread throughout the South. The Sunday School Board, recognizing its responsibility to help direct this growing interest of young people in the church, began in 1894 a special monthly paper for their use. Baptists in the South were anxious for the Baptist Young People's Union to become denominationally related. In 1918 it was dissolved at its own request, and a B.Y.P.U. Department was organized by the Sunday School Board.

2. Baptists and Higher Education

(1) *The Education Board.*—Southern Baptists were increasingly concerned about the educational opportunities available in Christian institutions. Numbers of colleges and universities had been established by Baptists in the South since the founding of the Convention. Many of them were owned or controlled by the state conventions or general associations, but the Southern Baptist Convention did not itself own or control any colleges. Nevertheless, the convention did show its interest in the Baptist colleges and other educational institutions when in 1913 it appointed a committee to study the advisability of establishing a board of education. Though such a board was not immediately forthcoming, the Education Commission was appointed in 1915.

The Commission, financed by an allocation from the Sunday School Board, sought in various ways to promote Christian higher education among Baptists. The work grew so rapidly that the commission recommended the creation of an education board. In 1919 the Convention established such a board at Birmingham, Alabama. The board sought to promote and strengthen Baptist schools. However, it was beset with many difficulties and was discontinued in 1928, when another education commission took its place.

(2) *Southern Baptist Theological Seminary.*—The seminary continued to prosper in the early years of this period, increasing in enrolment and influence. The last of the four professors who first taught in the seminary, President John A. Broadus, died in 1895. His successor, William H. Whitsitt, gave himself to the task of building up the student body. During his first year the enrolment rose to 318, the previous high having been 267. The future seemed bright indeed. However, serious controversy broke about the seminary, and particularly around Dr. Whitsitt. It was due to the Landmark contention that the validity of Baptist churches depends on a continuous chain of organized bodies in unbroken succession to New Testament time. According to this point of view, the churches in this chain practiced baptism and the Lord's Supper in a fashion essentially identical with that present-day Baptist churches.

From his intensive historical research at the British Museum and the libraries at Oxford and Cambridge, Dr. Whitsitt concluded that English Baptists restored immersion as the proper form of baptism in 1641. Immediately upon the publication of his conclusions, he and the Seminary were severely attacked. The controversy began in 1896 and continued until 1899, when Dr. Whitsitt resigned.

The controversy raised the issue of the Seminary's

relationship to the Convention. The legal title and control rested in the board of trustees, not the convention. Some wished to dissolve completely the tenuous arms that held the seminary and the convention together. However, with the resignation of Dr. Whitsitt and the election of Edgar Y. Mullins as president, these criticisms ceased, and the seminary resumed its progress.

(3) *Southwestern Baptist Theological Seminary.*— Southwestern Seminary was brought into being to meet the need of theological education for Baptist ministers in the great Southwest, where Baptist strength grew by leaps and bounds during the last half of the nineteenth century.

As early as 1841, when the Baptist movement in Texas was "no larger than a man's hand," Baptists there, feeling the need of an educated ministry, formed the Texas Baptist Education Society. In 1845, this society established the first Baylor University. It later united with Waco University but retained its name. B. H. Carroll established a theological department in 1901, and served as its dean.

Later, under Dr. Carroll's leadership, the Baylor Theological Seminary was established in 1905. In 1907 the Baptist General Convention of Texas approved the separation of the seminary from the university. Its charter, 1908, bore the name of Southwestern Baptist Theological Seminary. The institution moved to Fort Worth in 1910. After Dr. Carroll's death in 1914, L. R. Scarborough, the professor of evangelism, became president. The seminary belonged to the Baptist General Convention of Texas until 1926, when its ownership passed to the Southern Baptist Convention.

From the beginning, the Seminary received women on the same terms as men. In 1915, two new departments were established which were to lead in the next period to the development of two other schools within the seminary: the departments of religious education and of sacred music.

(4) *The Baptist Bible Institute.*—The Baptist Bible Institute, now the New Orleans Baptist Theological Seminary, was the first educational institution established by the direct participation of the Convention itself. Even in this instance, the institution was first established under the joint sponsorship of the Convention and several state conventions. (Southern and Southwestern seminaries had been established by friends of the Convention, but not by direct action of that body.)

The interest of the Convention in New Orleans was long-standing, for that area of the South represented a great missionary challenge to Baptists. The Institute's first session was in 1918, with Byron H. DeMent as its president.

III. THE CONVENTION AND SOCIAL CONCERN

1. *Care of the Sick*

Throughout the territory of the Southern Baptist Convention, state or community groups of Baptists began to erect hospitals. The Convention itself did not operate a hospital until it opened the Southern Baptist Hospital at New Orleans in 1926. However, long before this, the Convention became concerned about the problem of the Christian care of the ill. In 1917 it directed its committee on order of business to provide a place for the discussion of Baptist hospital work. In 1920, the Convention's El Paso Tuberculosis Sanatorium began operations. After some years the Convention discontinued it, and transferred the property to the Foreign Mission Board for use as a publishing house for Spanish religious literature.

2. Relief and Annuity Board

Concern for the problems faced by old and disabled ministers led the Convention to appoint a study commission in 1917. To the Convention at Hot Springs, Arkansas, in 1918 it recommended a Board of Ministerial Relief and Annuities. The Convention adopted the report and located it at Dallas, Texas.

3. Committee on Temperance and Social Service

The last decade of the nineteenth century and the early years of the twentieth were times of great social change. Increasing urbanization, growing industrialization, and mass immigration served to create new and complex social problems. The industrial worker was often exploited; the major portion of the material wealth was in the hands of comparatively few people, and traditional morality was weakening. Many Christians began to concern themselves with these conditions.

The problems were more acute in the North, but the South did not entirely escape them. Many Southern Baptists felt that the churches had a moral and social responsibility in these matters. What the Southern Baptist Convention could or should do about them became an object of concern.

The constitution of the Convention declared that it was "to promote Foreign and Domestic missions, and other important objects connected with the Redeemer's kingdom." Some questioned whether "other important objects connected with the Redeemer's kingdom" was broad enough to include social problems.

However, as the liquor problem became more serious, and public sentiment against beverage alcohol grew, the objections to the Convention's taking a stand on social issues declined. In 1907, a committee was appointed to arrange a mass meeting at the next annual session to consider some of the principal issues of the time. For several years thereafter a committee was appointed to report to the Convention on temperance.

In 1913, the Convention established the Social Service Commission to "deal with other such wrongs which cursed society. . . ." The commission made a remarkable report in 1914. After laying down the principles of Christian social action, it outlined the social task of the modern church. Some years later the committees on temperance and social service were combined into the Committee on Temperance and Social Service.

IV. Southern Baptists and the Christian World

Although Southern Baptists in this period came fully into their own as a great denomination, they were not unaffected by the growing demands for greater cooperation among denominational groups.

1. *The Baptist World Alliance*

About 1895 some Baptists began to think that there should be some kind of organization through which Baptists in all parts of the world might have fellowship and conferences pertaining to their mutual good. This new concern of Baptists began to take hold.

The Southern Baptist Convention, 1904, expressed a desire for a Pan-Baptist Conference "for the purpose of discussing matters of vital interest to the denomination," and appointed a committee to work with similar committees from other Baptist groups to arrange for such a conference. The committee reported in 1905 that a Baptist world conference was assured. The meeting convened in London July 11–19, 1905, and organized the Baptist World Alliance.

The Alliance recognized the independence of all churches, associations, and conventions, and asserted that its purpose was to demonstrate the essential oneness of Baptist churches throughout the world, and "to promote the spirit of fellowship, service, and cooperation among them. . . ."

2. *Interdenominational Co-operation*

Throughout this period the Convention was relatively favorably disposed toward that sentiment which developed in the denominations for greater co-operation among them.

Evidence of increasing co-operation came with the formation of the Foreign Missions Conference of North America and the Home Missions Council. The Convention left the Home Mission Board and the Foreign Mission Board free to determine their relationship with these bodies, but said that they should not in any way abridge their freedom of action or distort their policies. The Home Board did not relate itself in any fashion to the Home Missions Council, but the Foreign Mission Board found it wise and expedient to participate in the Foreign Missions Conference.

The Convention did not become one of the constituent bodies of the Federal Council of Churches of Christ in America (1908), but it took considerable interest in the invitation to participate in a world conference on faith and order. A request to arrange such a conference came to the convention in 1911. It referred the matter to a committee which reported annually to the Convention concerning the progress of the movement.

World War I delayed the plans for the world conference. By 1919 the Convention had so changed its attitude that the Commission on Faith and Order made no report. Instead, the Convention approved another committee's report which decried the various plans for federation and other forms of co-operation among denominations even though they might lead to only a partial surrender of Southern Baptist autonomy. Praising their denominationalism as being due to its loyalty to Christ and the Word, Southern Baptists effectively closed the door on what they regarded as "vague schemes of general co-operation with other Christian organizations."

SUGGESTED TOPICS FOR DISCUSSION

1. Suggest and discuss reasons for the rapid progress of Southern Baptists in this period.
2. Discuss the significance of Woman's Missionary Union to the work of the Convention.

I. MISSIONS IN HARD TIMES
1. Foreign Mission Board
2. Home Missions Weathers the Storm

II. EDUCATIONAL WORK OF THE CONVENTION
1. The Sunday School Board
2. The Convention and Higher Education

III. TENSIONS WITHIN THE CONVENTION
1. The Home Mission Board and the State Conventions
2. Controversy over Evolution

IV. INCREASING CO-ORDINATION AND CO-OPERATION
1. Development of the Cooperative Program
2. Executive Committee Enlarged and Strengthened
3. Hundred Thousand Club

V. EVANGELISM

7

A Time of Troubles

1920-1943

THE PERIOD 1920–1943 began auspiciously with the Seventy-five Million Campaign. There was high enthusiasm throughout the Convention, but the period proved to be one of trouble. The economic slump of 1921–22 caused the campaign to fall short of its goal in collections. The Convention, which had expanded its program at home and abroad on the basis of the pledges, quickly accumulated a serious debt. Furthermore, the treasurer of the Foreign Mission Board embezzled more than $100,000, and the treasurer of the Home Mission Board more than $900,000. The continued depression further weakened the economic capability of Southern Baptists. A controversy over evolution and bitter criticisms by enemies of the Convention in the 1920's made its work more difficult. World War II, which began in September, 1939, and involved the United States in 1941, greatly increased its problems.

During these twenty-three years, however, Southern Baptists made significant and solid gains in spite of all their troubles. For example, they increased from 3,199,005 in 1920 to 5,493,027 in 1943. Church property increased in value from about one hundred million to nearly two hundred-fifty million dollars, and total contributions nearly doubled. However, contributions to missionary, educational, and benevolent purposes were slightly less in 1943 than in 1920 because the Seventy-five Million Campaign was under way in 1920.

In spite of the large numerical increase between 1920 and 1943, the percentage of increase in membership went down significantly from the previous period. If Southern Baptists had continued to increase at the rate of the previous period, they would have had 7,053,400 members in 1943 instead of 5,493,027.

It would be a mistake, however, to underestimate the importance of this period, for, by the very nature of the times, Southern Baptists had to take stock of themselves and their situation, consolidate their gains, strengthen at their weak points, and develop a co-operative spirit they had not previously known. The phenomenal growth of Southern Baptists after 1943 would not have occurred apart from the solid foundations laid earlier.

I. MISSIONS IN HARD TIMES

1. Foreign Mission Board

With the close of World War I, Dr. J. F. Love, the corresponding secretary of the Foreign Mission Board, sought to inspire Southern Baptists to enlarge their mission program. "Not guns and soldiers now," he said, "but the gospel and missionaries are the means and agencies through which we must render our service to other nations." The appalling conditions in Europe especially concerned him. He and Dr. George W. Truett attended a conference on a Baptist program for Europe at London in 1920. Baptists from many countries met and planned how they might co-operate in relieving the widespread distress in Europe. Southern Baptists agreed to assume responsibility for five new fields: Spain, Yugoslavia, Hungary, Rumania, and portions of Russia. On their own, they also entered two new fields in the Near East: Palestine and Syria.

The Seventy-five Million Campaign, launched in 1919, seemed to be exceeding the fondest dreams of its promoters. Twenty of the seventy-five million dollars to be raised were to be spent on foreign missions. Presuming that it would receive these millions, the Foreign Mission Board doubled its work. Such stirring events occurred as the sailing of the *Empress of Japan* with eighty-four new missionaries aboard. But a recession reduced collections to about $58,500,000.

The Board could not quickly adjust its expenditures to its actual income, and was soon deeply in debt—more than a million dollars. Retrenchment became the order of the day. It sold some of its property, reduced its missionary force, and discontinued the services of many native missionaries. Furthermore, it faced a tragic situation: it could accept only a few of the host of young people who had volunteered for foreign mission work.

From Dr. Love's death, May, 1927, until late in 1929, the Board functioned without an executive secretary. T. B. Ray, field representative of the board, was in charge. In October, 1929, he became the executive secretary and served until Charles E. Maddry's election in October, 1932.

By 1933 the financial depression was at its worst. The Board's budget for 1933 was $200,000 less than for 1932, just over $600,000. Of that amount $65,000 had to be paid on interest. A tremendous crisis was at hand.

Fortunately, a financial turning point came in 1933 with the inauguration of the Baptist Hundred Thousand Club. Club members paid one dollar over and above their regular church offerings each month toward the retirement of Convention debts. Baptists were on their way back.

Dr. Maddry proved to be an energetic and effective secretary. The story of foreign mission achievements during his administration is too vast to be told here, but when he retired in 1944, the closing year of the first century of the Board's existence, there were regional secretaries for the great mission areas, stricter and more realistic qualifications for new missionaries, and renewed relations with the Foreign Missions Conference of North America. Southern Baptists had regained their confidence, and were once more looking forward with hope and assurance.

2. *Home Missions Weathers the Storm*

As was true throughout the Convention, optimism was unbounded in the Home Mission Board immediately after World War I. In 1920, convinced of continuing prosperity and increasing receipts, it enlarged its work more than 100 per cent. It appropriated nearly three million dollars in anticipation of its receipts. Then cotton prices dropped from forty to ten cents a pound —an example of what was happening to all commodities, wages, and income. This meant a sudden and calamitous deflation. Receipts of the board for 1921 were at an all-time high—$1,634,449.47—but more than one million dollars less than the appropriations for the year. It hurriedly contracted its overexpanded program, but expenditures exceeded receipts by $331,463.62. The receipts for 1922 were 33 per cent less than for 1921. By 1928, they were 40 per cent less. The decrease in work was at about the same ratio. The number of missionaries decreased from 1,656 in 1921 to 765 in 1928. There were 89 per cent fewer churches and mission stations being served. Baptisms decreased 69 per cent, and new churches begun decreased 65 per cent.

The Board's indebtedness increased yearly. By 1928 it was more than $1,500,000. The embezzlements of the treasurer through several years added more than $900,000 to the debt.

Southern Baptists, when they realized the tremendous crisis which the Board faced, designated November 11, 1928, as Honor Day, and gave nearly four hundred thousand dollars to help meet immediate needs. This proved the honor of the denomination, and helped to assure creditors of Baptist integrity.

Extensive investigation proved that no person except the treasurer was involved in the embezzlement, but a complete reorganization of the Board followed. Arch C. Cree, who became acting secretary, did heroic work in keeping the board from complete collapse and ruin. He led it in an effort, even at the cost of drastic curtailment of operations, to get the board from under its great burden of debt. It sought to relieve itself of further financial obligations relative to institutional experiments, and to concentrate more definitely on direct missionary work. This resulted in a gradual elimination of some of the mountain schools, and in moves that enabled it to get from under the financial burden of the El Paso Tuberculosis Sanatorium. It also discontinued co-operative mission work, done jointly with the state mission boards, except in strictly mission territory where a state board could not work by itself.

The Board reported to the Convention at New Orleans in 1930 that it had chosen J. B. Lawrence as executive secretary. He protested but accepted the responsibility, fully aware of the difficulties ahead. He set out to achieve the aims which the board had set up to retire the debt. It resolved to live within its income, even though that meant the reduction of its work. It also inaugurated a program to retire the entire indebtedness. It made further surveys of its tasks to be sure that its work would be in fields of greatest need.

Along with the other agencies and institutions of the Southern Baptist Convention, the Home Mission Board shared in the receipts of the Hundred Thousand Club, begun in 1933. The retirement of the debt was slow at first, but on May 12, 1943, Dr. Lawrence signed a check for fifty-five thousand dollars to pay the last debt of the board. This was both a financial and a moral victory for Southern Baptists, for every dollar they owed was paid in full, all other Convention debts having been previously paid.

While the Board was paying its debts, it again gradually enlarged its work. Its missionaries grew from 106 in 1929 to 489 in 1,037 mission stations in 1940. Lack of space makes it impossible to record the growth of these latter years, but the board's achievement proved again, as in the days of I. T. Tichenor, that it had not only been saved from disaster, but had again become a vital force in Southern Baptist life and progress.

II. Educational Work of the Convention

1. *The Sunday School Board*

With the passing, October 13, 1916, of J. M. Frost, the "Father of the Sunday School Board," its first era ended. Isaac J. Van Ness, who had for seventeen years been editorial secretary, took up where Dr. Frost left off. When he retired in June, 1935, Thomas Luther Holcomb succeeded him.

The Sunday School Board was not as radically affected by the several financial crises of the period as the other boards and institutions of the Convention, for it was an income producing board. Naturally, during the depression, its receipts from the sales of its publications decreased. However, it was able to make helpful contributions from its earnings to other causes while doing its own work. Besides caring for the expenses of the Executive Committee, the Promotion Committee, and fixed Convention expenses, it made contributions to the seminaries, the Brotherhood, and other Southern Baptist enterprises. When the Hundred Thousand Club was organized, it bore its expenses so that all its proceeds could be applied to Convention debts.

The Sunday School Board spent its formative childhood under the watchful eye of Frost. It grew into young adulthood under Van Ness, and developed into maturity under Holcomb.

When the Board began in 1891, many handicaps had to be overcome, among them a fear by many that the board, if it became strong, might interfere with the rights of the churches. Dr. Frost soon allayed these fears. From the first, as its earnings permitted, the board made appropriations to the several states for the promotion of Sunday school work. They selected the workers and planned the work. The board's policy was co-operative, not authoritative.

By 1900, it was evident that the Board could improve Sunday schools by inaugurating a program of training for teachers. Its first field worker was B. W. Spilman, North Carolina, in 1901. Several others followed in the next eight years. In 1910, Prince E. Burroughs, Texas, became secretary in charge of teacher training. (He served the board until his retirement in June, 1943.)

Dr. Frost led the Board from weakness to strength. He won for it the united support of Southern Baptists, and led it to complete success in its long and arduous struggle with the American Baptist Publication Society for the patronage of Southern Baptists. His successors had many problems with the growing institution, but they did not have to struggle to keep it alive and save it from forces that would have destroyed it.

The increasing emphasis in the Convention upon co-operative activity and organizational and promotional efficiency made it possible for Dr. Van Ness to expand the Nashville organization. By 1922, the number of field departments in Nashville had risen from one to six. Five more departments were added in the next five years. Thus while the Board was achieving adulthood, Nashville was becoming the center of a strong organizational, promotional, and educational institution.

Among the numerous important developments, per—haps none was more important than the development of the department of Sunday school administration. Un der the leadership of layman Arthur Flake, Mississippi, the methods for Sunday school enlargement were perfected. The Sunday school became not only a church teaching agency, but also an effective agency for church efficiency and promotion.

The Board intensified its efforts for more and better Sunday schools, and also became active in several related fields of service. As has been noted, the Convention in 1917, by request of the Baptist Young People's Union of the South, committed to it the B.Y.P.U. work. The next year it established the B.Y.P.U. Department and selected Landrum P. Leavell as its secretary, who served until his death in 1929, when Jerry E. Lambdin succeeded him.

In 1924, because of a growing interest in Vacation Bible schools, the Board established a Vacation Bible School Department and elected Homer L. Grice, Georgia, as secretary and also editor of the V.B.S. textbooks. He served until his retirement January 1, 1953.

In 1921 the Convention established for its boards the Inter-Board Commission on Student Religious Activity and located it at Memphis. Frank H. Leavell, Mississippi, became its secretary and served until his death, December 7, 1949. By general agreement, the Board assumed responsibility for this work and moved it to Nashville in 1926 and changed the name to the Baptist Student Union Department.

In 1929 the Board, by action of the Convention, assumed responsibility for the summer programs of Ridgecrest Baptist Assembly, then owned by the Convention. The Convention had come into possession of Ridgecrest, begun in 1907, and was doing well with it until the Convention mortgaged it for other denominational debts, caused largely by the debts of the depression years. In 1944, the Convention transferred the property to the board and made it possible for it to begin a program of development that in a few years made it a great training center for all the Convention's boards and commissions, and the Woman's Missionary Union.

During the administration of Dr. T. L. Holcomb the Sunday School Board sought through a carefully designed program of promotion to carry its educational program to every church in the Convention. Soon after he went to the board from Oklahoma City in 1935, he launched the Five-year Sunday School Board Promotional Program. It employed the district association as a promotional unit, and was so successful that at its conclusion a new Four-year Promotional Program was undertaken for 1941–1944.

The rapid multiplication of agencies and institutions in the Convention, and their increasing complexity, led the Convention in 1937 to appoint a committee on co-ordination and correlation. Within the Sunday School Board this same need for co-ordination and correlation was felt. In 1939 the board reorganized its various departments into three divisions: business management, editorial service, and education and promotion.

Thus, in the period under our consideration, the Sunday School Board moved forward rapidly, finding the time of troubles less troublesome to it than to the other boards and institutions of the Convention. By the end of the period, it had become so closely related to the churches that they were reminded every Sunday of its significant existence through their use of its literature, its methods and organizations of promotion, and the spirit it engendered.

2. *The Convention and Higher Education*

During 1919–1943 the educational institutions of the Southern Baptist Convention, and also of the state conventions, fared much like the Convention agencies. In the early years of the period there was continued expansion and growth, but the depression brought serious crises to the colleges and the seminaries. Some of the colleges closed, but the seminaries and most of the colleges survived, even though, in many instances, faculty salaries went unpaid for periods, and indebtedness climbed as the student bodies decreased.

The Convention created the Education Board in 1919, and discontinued it in 1928, when it created the Education Commission. The Education Commission, during most of the succeeding years of the period, was greatly hampered by a small, and for a time, almost non-existent budget. There were no salaried officers, and no headquarters office. The commission was largely composed of denominational college presidents, whose devotion to their task kept it going.

The Convention, in this time of trouble, did not launch any new educational institutions. A partial exception to this statement was the American Baptist Theological Seminary, founded in Nashville, Tennessee, in 1924, and supported jointly by the National Baptist Convention and the Southern Baptist Convention. This seminary for Negro Baptist ministerial students was constantly beset by difficulties, and even at the end of the period had only forty-three students.

The Southern Baptist Seminary was under the leadership of the wise and able E. Y. Mullins until his death in 1928. During his administration, the endowment significantly increased, the student body grew, and the seminary moved in 1926 from downtown Louisville to its new campus, The Beeches, one of the most beautiful seminary campuses in the country.

John R. Sampey became the president just as the financial crash and depression overwhelmed the nation. The Seminary soon had a debt of nearly one million dollars, and a decreased student body. However, before Dr. Sampey retired in 1942, the indebtedness was nearly paid and the student body was once more growing rapidly.

Dr. L. R. Scarborough was president of Southwestern Baptist Theological Seminary until his death in 1942. Dr. E. D. Head succeeded him. Though it was also beset by critical financial difficulties during the depression, it was out of debt by the end of 1943 and had an enrolment of nearly one thousand.

The Baptist Bible Institute in New Orleans, at first jointly owned by the Southern Baptist Convention and the Mississippi and the Louisiana state conventions, passed fully into Southern Baptist Convention ownership in 1925. The first president of the Institute, Dr. B. H. DeMent, was succeeded by W. W. Hamilton in 1928, who served until 1942.

The Woman's Missionary Union Training School at Louisville continued under the ownership and control of the Woman's Missionary Union. In 1941 it moved from downtown Louisville to a campus adjoining that of Southern Seminary.

III. Tensions Within the Convention

1. *The Home Mission Board and the State Conventions*

From time to time, due usually to misunderstandings, conflicts of interest developed between the Home Mission Board and some of the state conventions. They were due largely to the fact that the Home Mission Board worked in states that had their own conventions.

The Convention sought more than once to define clearly the relation between it and other Baptist bodies. It made its chief statement in 1923 and repeated it in 1924. It set forth the principles that the convention bears an advisory relationship only to all other Baptist bodies and has no authority over them, that the sphere of convention work is in conflict with no other organization or interest of the denomination, and that "where the activities of the Convention are related to the activities of other Baptist bodies the controlling principle is free and voluntary co-operation for common ends." The statement also said that no other general Baptist body has any authority over the convention, and that the principle of self-determination operates in all cases. Co-operation, it said, will be "not by coercion, but by mutual consent. Free conference and frank discussion enable us to reach satisfactory conclusions for co-operative work. We must never convert moral and spiritual into legal relations among Baptist general bodies."

2. *Controversy over Evolution*

"Modernism" was a troublesome issue in other denominations during the 1920's, but Southern Baptists were little disturbed by it, having set themselves squarely against it. The only related problem that really disturbed them was a difference of opinion on the subject of evolution. By 1924, some felt that the Convention should take a strong stand against it. Others felt that such a statement would undermine the complete freedom of scientific investigation and discussion that should exist in Southern Baptist colleges. The sessions at Memphis in 1925 and Houston in 1926 were stormy. At Houston the Convention adopted a statement on evolution made by its president, George W. McDaniel, which reaffirmed its acceptance of the teachings of Genesis. The strife died down quickly. The depression, the reappearance of the prohibition issue, certain changes in leadership, and the decline of controversy in the Convention, all served to restore harmony.

As one result of the controversy, in 1928 the Convention made a long and detailed statement regarding its relations to other Baptist bodies. Like its predecessors, it asserted the voluntary principle of organization and the autonomy of all Baptist bodies.

IV. INCREASING CO-ORDINATION AND CO-OPERATION

The organization of an executive committee of the Convention in 1917, and the launching of the Seventy-five Million Campaign in 1919, symbolized the increasing desire within the Convention for a co-ordination of its functions and more co-operation by Southern Baptists in its great world evangelistic and missionary program. It was ten years, however, before the Executive Committee became a potent force in the Convention.

1. *Development of the Cooperative Program*

In part the financial failure of the Seventy-five Million Campaign was the cause of developments so significant and far-reaching as to be, perhaps, the key to the more recent phenomenal progress and enlargement of the Convention. When the Seventy-five Million Campaign was launched, a commission, known as the Campaign Commission, was appointed. A year later it was replaced by the Conservation Commission, which kept before the Convention the necessity of stewardship promotion, evangelism, and co-operation. The campaign also made Southern Baptists conscious of the need of careful budgeting and planning in their future operations, and led the Convention, in 1923 to appoint a committee "On the Future Program of Southern Baptists."

The next year the commission recommended a simultaneous every-member canvass in every Baptist church. It emphasized the need for permanency in the Convention's financial plans through adherence to "Bible principles of stewardship and tithing." It also expressed the hope that, instead of designating gifts, individuals and churches would make contributions to the whole program. It recommended a general committee, with headquarters in Nashville, to promote the program, and each year recommended to the Convention a budget for the following year, with allocations to each object of the Convention by percentages. The Convention approved the recommendations of the commission and its request that the boards and agencies should present written statements of their needs for the coming year so that the commission could be properly informed as it sought to make a Convention budget.

Repeatedly the Future Program Commission, the official name of the committee appointed in 1923, stated that systematic giving and co-operation were the solutions to the tasks of Southern Baptists. In 1925, the Convention changed the name of the commission to Commission on Cooperative Program of Southern Baptists and officially adopted the Cooperative Program.

2. *Executive Committee Enlarged and Strengthened*

Increasing emphasis in American life on business efficiency led the Convention to study its own work to see if it could increase its efficiency. A business efficiency committee was appointed; and in its 1927 report, it recommended that the work done by the Cooperative Program Commission be taken over by the Executive Committee, and that the Executive Committee, joined by all Convention officials, should be the Convention's promotional agency. The Executive Committee was enlarged, and its duties and functions were expanded and defined. With the election of Austin Crouch as its executive secretary, the Executive Committee in 1927 began to function as the ad interim agency of the Convention.

It would be difficult to overestimate the significance of the Cooperative Program and the strengthening of the Executive Committee in relation to the progress of Southern Baptists.

3. *Hundred Thousand Club*

The Executive Committee began to make itself felt, but the financial condition in the country in the early

1930's discouraged even the most optimistic. The great debt of the Convention hung like a pall over its life. In 1933, when things seemed to be at their worst, the Baptist Hundred Thousand Club proved to be the salvation of the situation. In 1936, James E. Dillard became director of promotion for the Cooperative Program and the Hundred Thousand Club. Under his leadership, "Debt Free in '43" came to pass, for every debt was paid in full.

V. EVANGELISM

From its organization in 1845, the Southern Baptist Convention, definitely evangelistic, never neglected soul-winning, even in times of trouble. When it planned to raise seventy-five million dollars it also planned to reap a great harvest of souls. Connected with the great effort to pay off the Convention's debt in the latter 1930's and early 1940's were evangelistic campaigns. The Convention endorsed the Southwide Baptist Revival in 1938. In 1940 Southern Baptists joined with other Baptists in a nation-wide Baptist evangelistic crusade, and continued it in 1941 as the Southwide Soul-Winning Crusade. Then plans were projected for the great Centennial Evangelistic Crusade in 1944.

Baptists were seeking to keep level the great tripod which had given them strength—namely, missions, evangelism, and education.

SUGGESTIONS FOR DISCUSSION

1. What actions, if any, should the Convention have taken to forestall the heavy debt?
2. Discuss the work of the Executive Committee.

CHAPTER 8 OUTLINE

I. Advance in Missions
   1. Foreign Mission Board
   2. Home Mission Board
   3. Woman's Missionary Union
   4. Baptist Brotherhood

II. Progress in Education
   1. The Sunday School Board
   2. Seminary Education
   3. Education Commission

III. The Convention and Social Concern
   1. The Care of the Aged and Ill
   2. The Christian Life Commission
   3. Baptist Joint Committee on Public Affairs

IV. Historical Interests of Southern Baptists

V. Radio and Television Commission

VI. The Developing Organization and Life of The Convention
   1. Organizational Revision and Changes
   2. Expansion of Territory
   3. Relations with Other Religious Bodies
   4. Signs of Vitality

VII. Retrospect and Prospect

8

Prosperity and Progress

1944-1957

WE ARE TOO CLOSE to the period 1944–1957 fully to understand it or to see it in perspective. Nevertheless, it can be said confidently that it has been a period of progress and prosperity. The Convention has shared with the whole nation the stimulus of the postwar boom and the consequent expansion in all fields of endeavor. Most would agree that there has been a real revival of religion in these years. Southern Baptists have contributed to it and have profited from it.

The optimism and confidence which characterized the last decade of the nineteenth century and the first two decades of this one have once more become the heritage of Southern Baptists. They believe that the time of troubles is behind, and look forward to still greater achievements.

I. ADVANCE IN MISSIONS

1. Foreign Mission Board

When the period opened, the country was still in the throes of World War II. It particularly affected the work of the Foreign Mission Board in both the Orient and Europe. Nevertheless, work went on behind the Japanese lines in China, and reports of faithfulness in war-torn Europe filtered through to the board. Active in relief work, it reported that Baptists gave approximately a million dollars to world emergency relief in 1942 and 1943.

Though war was still raging, 1944 marked the beginning of a new era for the Foreign Mission Board. M. Theron Rankin became executive secretary, and the board began to consider carefully the needs of the postwar world. Its total income in 1944, exclusive of relief funds, was nearly three million dollars, and was an increase of more than a half million dollars over 1943.

As soon as the war ended, missionaries returned to the Orient. A few years later the Communists expelled all Baptist missionaries from China.

Two events of great significance to missions were, first, the new policy, adopted by the Convention in 1946, providing specifically for the capital needs of its agencies, and second, the Advance Program of Foreign Missions which was recommended by the Foreign Mission Board and adopted in principle by the Southern Baptist Convention in 1949. The goal of the Advance Program was 1,750 overseas missionaries, and an annual over-all budget of ten million dollars.

Recognizing the challenge of such a program, the 1950 Convention allotted to the Foreign Mission Board all the Cooperative Program funds received above the Convention's operating budget, and the six and one-half millions which were distributed among all of the agencies and institutions of the Convention. Similar action was taken the following year, when all receipts above seven million dollars went to the Foreign Mission Board. After 1951, the Foreign Board received 75 per cent, and the Home Mission Board 25 per cent, of the gifts over and above the funds regularly budgeted for all of the agencies. This plan meant that in 1956 the Foreign Mission Board received through the Cooperative Program $2,407,709.63 in addition to the $3,800,000 which it received through the regular budgeted item for operating expenses and capital needs. The regular receipts and the designated gifts and special offerings gave the board total receipts of $12,738,681 in 1956, or more than four times what it received in 1944. Its work also increased in much the same way. The approximately five hundred missionaries assigned to nineteen national areas in 1944 increased to more than 1,100 missionaries assigned to thirty-eight countries in 1956.

The untimely death of Dr. Rankin in 1953 brought a sense of loss to Southern Baptists everywhere. He was the first missionary to serve as the Board's executive secretary. In October, 1953, Baker James Cauthen, secretary to the Orient, succeeded Dr. Rankin.

2. Home Mission Board

The Home Mission Board, like the other boards and agencies of the Convention, was enlarging its work at the beginning of this period. Its debts were fully paid in 1943. Increased receipts permitted it rapidly to expand its work. In 1944, for example, it appointed 153 new missionaries, opened 82 new mission stations, and bought 54 places for mission activities. Its receipts that year were $1,174,699.

In 1944 the Board re-established its department of evangelism and assumed responsibility for directing the evangelistic centennial crusade. Its work was organized to care for these departments: Education; Work among the Indians, Foreigners, and Language Groups; Cuban Missions; Work in the Canal Zone and Panama; the City Mission Program; the Country Church; Co-operative Work with Negroes; Camp Work and Defense Communities; Jewish Work; the Department of Evangelism; and the Church Building Loan Fund.

Increasing migration by the people within the country, especially during and after World War II, included many thousand Southern Baptists who moved into the urban areas of the West and much of the midwest and the North. In 1946 the Board chose a field secretary for the West, and called the work "pioneer missions." By 1956, this work was being conducted in twenty-five states from the West coast as far east as Pennsylvania and New York.

The department of evangelism, C. E. Matthews, director, led Southern Baptists into a series of simultaneous revivals throughout the country, and into the greatest evangelistic period in Southern Baptist history.

The Board began its Five-year Crusade in Home Missions in 1950. It was so successful that it was followed by the Four-year Conquest for Christ program. In 1956, it employed 1,180 missionaries from its receipts of above $4,000,000. Dr. Lawrence, who became secretary in 1929, retired in 1953. Courts Redford succeeded him.

3. *Woman's Missionary Union*

The Woman's Missionary Union continued as an auxiliary to the Southern Baptist Convention, though its auxiliary status in no way diminished its influence in and contribution to the Convention. Under the leadership of its executive secretary, Miss Kathleen Mallory, and her successor, Miss Alma Hunt, it nearly doubled its membership.

4. Baptist Brotherhood

In 1944 the Baptist Brotherhood of the South was a standing committee in the Convention, but in 1951 it was elevated to the status of a commission. Its growth and increasing influence were remarkable. By 1956, there were nearly eleven thousand church brotherhoods with over four hundred thousand members.

II. PROGRESS IN EDUCATION

1. The Sunday School Board

The phenomenal growth of the Southern Baptist Convention since 1944 has been paced by the growth of the Sunday School Board. Not only have its functions and services been ever enlarging, but the results of its efforts have been spectacular. For example, during 1944–1956 Sunday school enrolment more than doubled, increasing to 6,823,713. Training Union enrolment more than tripled. The total Sunday school and Training Union study course awards increased more than threefold, or to nearly one and a half million awards in 1956. The board's receipts from all sources increased several times over. In 1956, its net sales amounted to more than twenty-one million dollars.

The Board greatly enlarged its physical plant, developed a new assembly at Glorieta, New Mexico, and added Baptist Book Stores until there were fifty of them in 1956. In addition, new periodicals and books continued to pour from its presses, and audio-visual aids became a significant part of its productions.

T. L. Holcomb, who became executive secretary-treasurer in June, 1935, retired in June, 1953. James L. Sullivan succeeded him. Under Dr. Sullivan's leadership the Board made a complete study of its functions, policies, and organization. As a result it changed its administrative organization into four divisions: merchandise and sales, education, service, and business.

The greatest asset of the Board was not physical properties, however, but the continued confidence and support of the churches, and their use of its materials and methods. This was reflected not only in the sales of its publications, but also in the rapid growth of the educational units and plants of Southern Baptist churches and the increasing emphasis of the churches upon religious education. The significant increase of employed personnel devoting their time to the educational program of the churches was further proof of its effective leadership.

2. *Seminary Education*

The rapid growth of Southern Baptists, and the improved effectiveness of their work, created a great demand for pastors, educational directors, ministers of music, and other trained full-time church workers. This made an enlargement of existing seminaries and the creation of new ones necessary. As a result, enrolment in all the seminaries increased from 2,279 in 1943–44 to 6,373 in 1956–57. In addition, the Seminary Extension Department enrolled more than 7,000 in 1957.

In 1950, the Convention accepted Golden Gate Baptist Theological Seminary at Berkeley, California, from Southern Baptists in the West, and voted to establish Southeastern Baptist Theological Seminary at Wake Forest, North Carolina. Both seminaries grew rapidly. Golden Gate enrolled 348 students in 1956–57, and Southeastern, 681. Harold K. Graves succeeded B. C. Herring as the president of Golden Gate, and Sydnor C. Stealey became the first president of Southeastern.

Miss Carrie U. Littlejohn, for years president of the Woman's Missionary Union Training School, retired in 1951, to be succeeded by Miss Emily K. Lansdell. In 1954 the name of the school was changed to Carver School of Missions and Social Work. In 1957, the ownership and control of the school passed into the hands of the Southern Baptist Convention.

In 1957 the Southern Baptist Convention voted to establish a new seminary, to be called the Midwestern Baptist Theological Seminary. Dr. Millard J. Berquist was elected the first president.

During this period the existing seminaries continued to grow and to enlarge their curricula. Southern Baptist Seminary under Dr. Fuller's leadership founded a school of church music in 1944, and in 1953 Dr. Fuller's successor, Duke K. McCall, led in founding a school of religious education.

Southwestern Seminary during this period grew from just under one thousand students to well over two thousand, making it the largest seminary in the world. Every Southern Baptist seminary changed administration during this period, and Southwestern was no exception. Dr. Head retired as president in 1953 and was succeeded by J. Howard Williams.

The Baptist Bible Institute was given permission to change its name to the New Orleans Baptist Theological Seminary, in 1946. That same year Dr. Duke McCall was succeeded as president by Roland Q. Leavell. Perhaps the most notable development in the life of New Orleans Seminary has been its removal to a new, beautiful, and functional campus on the outskirts of New Orleans. This was one of the significant achievements of the capital needs program of Southern Baptists.

The Convention continued to co-operate with the National Baptist Convention of U.S.A., Incorporated, in the support of the American Baptist Theological Seminary at Nashville.

3. Education Commission

The work of the Education Commission was considerably enlarged during this period. This was notably true after the end of World War II and the rapid increase of enrolment in Southern Baptist colleges. The budget of the Education Commission was enlarged, and in 1951 R. Orin Cornett became the first executive secretary of the commission, with offices at Nashville. The expansion of services of the Education Commission had been fostered by the Southern Association of Baptist Colleges and Schools, which was organized at a meeting of Baptist college presidents in 1948.

III. The Convention and Social Concern

1. The Care of the Aged and Ill

The Relief and Annuity Board continued to consolidate its position and to strengthen its annuity plans.

Though relief continued to be an item of considerable size, the emphasis in this period was educating churches and pastors to participate in its annuity programs.

In addition to operating the Southern Baptist Hospital in New Orleans, which became a Convention agency in 1926, the Convention briefly managed the Baptist Hospital in San Antonio, Texas. Then, toward the close of the period, it began to operate a new hospital at Jacksonville, Florida, known as Baptist Memorial Hospital. The major work of Southern Baptists in caring for the ill, however, was still in the hands of the hospitals owned and operated by state conventions.

2. *The Christian Life Commission*

The Social Service Commission, guided for a number of years by its chairman, Jesse B. Weatherspoon, professor in the Southern Baptist Theological Seminary, was given funds in 1947 to provide for an executive secretary. Hugh A. Brimm served until 1953, when A. C. Miller succeeded him. Under Dr. Miller the offices were moved from Louisville to Nashville, Tennessee, and the name changed to Christian Life Commission.

One of the most controversial issues to come before Southern Baptists in this period was precipitated by the Supreme Court's decision declaring race segregation in the public schools to be unconstitutional. In 1954 the Convention, after considerable debate, approved the statement of the Christian Life Commission recognizing the Supreme Court decision as being "in harmony with the constitutional guarantee of equal freedom to all citizens, and with the Christian principles of equal justice and love for all men."

3. *Baptist Joint Committee on Public Affairs*

Baptists have historically been vigilant in their defense of religious freedom and the principle of separation of church and state. Beginning in 1946, they have had representation on the Baptist Joint Committee on Public Affairs "to enunciate, commend, and defend the historic Baptist principle of religious freedom with particular application to the separation of church and state as embodied in the Constitution of the United States."

The Southern Baptist Convention and the American Baptist Convention established this committee. Four other Baptist groups in the United States then associated themselves with it. Until his retirement in 1950, J. M. Dawson was executive secretary, with headquarters at Washington, D.C. C. Emanuel Carlson, of the American Baptist Convention, succeeded him.

IV. Historical Interests of Southern Baptists

Southern Baptists, a relatively young denomination, did not become vitally interested in preserving and writing its history until comparatively recent times. From time to time during the nineteenth century, the Convention adopted resolutions encouraging Baptist historical efforts, but relatively little was accomplished until the organization of the Southern Baptist Historical Society at Louisville, Kentucky, in 1938, when a Kentucky charter was granted to it.

In 1947, the Convention gave the Society the status of a commission and so recognized it until 1951, when it created the Historical Commission and Norman W. Cox became its secretary. (The society became auxiliary to the Commission.) During these years the Sunday School Board offered to furnish quarters for both the commission and its library. Upon the completion of the Board's eleven-story office building on Ninth Avenue, the commission moved into the building. Its library was integrated with the Board's Dargan Library and the name changed to the Dargan-Carver Library, thereby honoring Dr. W. O. Carver, the real founder of both the Historical Society and the Historical Commission.

With ampler appropriations from the Convention, and in its new position, the Commission's services to churches, colleges, universities, and seminaries rapidly increased, among them microfilming of rare books and documents of all kinds and making films available to all who wished to purchase them.

The Commission, after months of conferences with all Baptist agencies of every kind, completed plans for the writing and publishing of the two-volume *Southern Baptist Encyclopedia* of 1,700 pages. The Sunday School Board published it and began its sale in early 1958. It required five years, 57 editors. and 899 writers to prepare its varied contents.

V. RADIO AND TELEVISION COMMISSION

In 1938 the Convention appointed a committee of seven, with Samuel F. Lowe of Georgia as chairman, to study the advisability of the denomination's making use of the radio. The committee was reappointed yearly as a special committee. In its earlier years it labored almost without funds, but was able to report in 1941 that it had begun a Baptist hour network.

In 1944 a permanent radio committee was established, and authorized to employ the necessary leadership to provide for the work committed to it.

The increasing demands and work of the radio committee led the Convention to create the Radio Commission in 1946. Dr. Lowe, who had been associated with the radio work of the Convention from the beginning, served as the director of this commission until his death in 1952. At that time the Baptist Hour was carried by more than 330 stations in twenty-eight states. The commission was also distributing a transcription library and had begun to study the needs in the television field.

Under the new director, Paul M. Stevens, the Commission's name was was changed to the Radio and Television Commission, and its headquarters was moved from Atlanta, Georgia, to Fort Worth, Texas.

VI. THE DEVELOPING ORGANIZATION AND LIFE OF THE CONVENTION

1. *Organizational Revision and Changes*

As the Convention grew in size and complexity, it became necessary from time to time to revise and enlarge the organization. A complete revision of the constitution and bylaws of the Convention was ordered in 1942, but it was not until 1946 that it was adopted. Though some revision took place afterwards, they were not substantially changed.

The revised constitution broadened the stated purpose of the Convention to conform to the more complex work of the Convention and to give ample legal ground for all the various types of work done by the Convention. Among the most important changes was one which limited the tenure of members of boards and of the Executive Committee to two three-year terms. Another important change sought to give the states a more proportional representation on boards. In 1953 the Executive Committee was enlarged in similar fashion. In addition, the sad experience of the past dictated changes in the bylaws to improve the methods and safeguard handling money and securities.

While the Convention was struggling to pay off the indebtedness of its agencies, it adopted a business and financial plan "to give assurance to the contributors to the work of the Convention and its agencies that everything humanly possible will be done to avoid debts, and . . . to acquaint the denomination with the business methods of the Convention and its agencies." This plan, adopted in 1939, served until 1947, when it was revised to define the manner in which agencies of the Convention are, or may be, financed and how they are to handle funds and make reports. The Executive Committee was given broad powers to study the financial operations of any of the agencies and, on the basis of its reports, to recommend a budget to the Convention.

In 1946, the Convention approved the recommendation of the Executive Committee that a capital needs budget be added to the annual operating budgets of the agencies. In recent years the Convention has divided money received beyond the budget as follows: 75 per cent to the Foreign Mission Board and 25 per cent to the Home Mission Board. The provision of a capital needs budget was a significant development in the history of Southern Baptist agencies, and an important advance in the Cooperative Program.

The Executive Committee, which took on new importance in 1927, continued to grow in influence in this period. Dr. Austin Crouch, the first executive secretary of the committee, continued to serve until his retirement in 1946. From then until 1951, Duke K. McCall filled the position. Porter Routh succeeded him.

From 1927 until 1946 the Executive Committee served as the administrator of all funds and legacies given to the Southern Baptist Convention. In 1946, the Convention created the Southern Baptist Foundation to encourage the making of gifts to the various objects of the Convention, and to serve the Convention and its agencies as the administrator of funds they intrusted to it. By 1957 the holdings of the foundation amounted to nearly three million dollars.

2. Expansion of Territory

The rapid movement of Baptists from the South into the West and the North, and the desire of numerous churches in these areas to affiliate with the Southern Baptist Convention, briefly perplexed the Convention. However, it soon put aside any hesitation it may have had, and began to admit as constituent bodies state conventions that had previously been outside of what had been regarded by many as the territory of the Southern Baptist Convention. The Southern Baptist General Convention of California was admitted in 1942. Other Southern Baptist state conventions were soon recognized: Kansas in 1948; Oregon-Washington in 1949; and Colorado in 1956.

The pressure of the western movement forced the Convention to redefine its position relative to territorial limitations. This it did in 1944 and 1949. In 1951 it again reaffirmed its position that the Southern Baptist Convention had no national territorial limitations and that its boards and agencies were "free to serve as a source of blessing to any community or any people anywhere in the United States."

3. *Relations with Other Religious Bodies*

While the Convention was including a larger portion of the United States, it again firmly rejected any move to relate itself with any of the ecumenical agencies or organizations. It refused to send an observer to the constitutive sessions of the World Council of Churches in 1948. More than once its committee on common problems with Northern Baptists, which in 1949 became the committee on relations with other religious bodies, reaffirmed opposition to any ties with ecumencial bodies.

4. *Signs of Vitality*

In spite of all the organizational changes the Convention made during this period, its rapid expansion and developing complexity led many to feel that a study of the whole program of Southern Baptists, done carefully and wisely, would prove of value in planning for more effective work. In 1956, the Convention appointed a committee to study the total Southern Baptist program and gave it authority to employ any professional assistance it deemed wise. Thus, it continued to demonstrate its vitality and its willingness to keep its organization flexible enough to meet new needs.

As another evidence of its continuing vitality, the Convention adopted a program in 1956 suggested by its president, C. C. Warren, to undertake the addition of 10,000 new churches and 20,000 missions before the celebration of the Convention's third jubilee in 1964.

Perhaps the most important emphases of this period of progress and prosperity were upon evangelism and stewardship. In 1944, the Centennial Crusade was launched with major emphasis upon an evangelistic effort to win one million souls to Christ in 1945, and carry on a Southwide stewardship revival. While the goal of the Centennial Crusade was not reached, a renewed interest in soul-winning was felt in the Convention. Gifts to Convention objects rose significantly. A strong emphasis on the tithe as a minimum standard for Christian stewardship also became characteristic of the Convention's promotional activities.

The campaign to add a million members to the Sunday schools of Southern Baptist churches in 1954 was followed by a great simultaneous evangelistic crusade in 1955. Though the goal of "A Million More in '54" was not reached, nearly six hundred thousand new members were enrolled in the Sunday schools. As a result of the simultaneous revival crusade and other activities, 1955 proved to be the greatest year for evangelism in Southern Baptist history. Over four hundred thousand converts were baptized.

As the period closed, the Convention was making plans and looking forward to a great nation-wide evangelistic crusade in co-operation with other Baptist bodies in the United States to be called the Baptist Jubilee Advance, 1959–64. This five-year program of advance was planned to culminate on the date of the one hundred and fiftieth anniversary of the organization

of Baptist work on a national level through the Triennial Convention in 1814.

VII. Retrospect and Prospect

The facts recited in this book about Southern Baptists
speak for themselves. Nevertheless, a few concluding
observations may be in order.

First, it appears clear what a genuine concern for
missions, evangelism, and education created co-
operative work among the Baptists of the South and
kept them together.

Another factor in the remarkable unity which has
characterized Southern Baptists is that the Convention
emphasized the practical aspects of its mission and did
not concern itself with dogmatically defining doctrine
and polity for the churches. Apart from that caused by
Landmarkism, no large defections from the Convention
have taken place.

A third factor in the cohesive nature of Southern
Baptists was the homogeneity of the people and area
principally served by the Convention. The social structure of the South has had an affinity with what Southern
Baptists have tried to do. The South has been less
eroded by the "acids of modernity"; there has been less
secularization of life; and there has been no major
immigration into the South since 1845.

Though the standard of education among Southern
Baptist ministers, taken as a whole, has never been high,
the Convention has been fortunate in having a well-
educated leadership throughout its life. Though this
leadership has never disparaged the men who were not
fortunate enough to obtain a high level of education, it

has provided a good leaven to generate progress, growth, and unity.

Another major factor in the life of the Southern Baptist Convention was the tension always present between centralization on one hand and decentralization on the other. Both viewpoints were expressed in the original constitution of the Convention in 1845, and throughout the history of the convention these two emphases have been prominent. The local church was emphasized but so was the co-operative, over-all, general point of view. On the whole this has been healthy, and normally a fine harmony and balance have been achieved. Nevertheless, these tendencies sometimes led to conflicts.

Southern Baptists have always sought to find a common denominator among their people, to make the message simple and, perhaps, to look askance at those who would suggest that oversimplification can be dangerous. As a consequence, on occasion, tension developed between segments of the Convention and the educational agencies and institutions of Southern Baptists. Nevertheless, simplicity in presenting the claims of Christ has been one of the major factors in the growth of the people.

With the partial exception of the Negro, Southern Baptist life and influence have spanned all social divisions and levels. This has been a source of tremendous power and influence. The rich and the poor, the lowly and the great, the educated and uneducated, all have found a place for themselves in Southern Baptist life.

Untold benefits have come to the Convention from agencies and institutions not organically related to the Convention, most of which, because of the limitations necessarily imposed on this short story, have not been discussed here. For example, in addition to state conventions and Baptist colleges, to which brief references have been made, there is the incalculable contribution of the state Baptist papers. These have, through the years, helped form an opinion favorable to the Convention and its work. Its editors have had the ears and hearts of the so-called grass roots more, perhaps, than any other single group of people. These papers have constituted the forum in which policy has been wrought out democratically. In addition, the local association has been the unit closest to the church and has constituted a most powerful influence. But to explore these influences fully would require the writing of a history of the Baptists of the South, which is a far more ambitious work than this brief history of Southern Baptists.

The examination of the history of Southern Baptists would reveal that the fathers cultivated well and laid out the framework for a truly general organization for Baptist work in the South. However, it was not until the 1890's and after that the Convention became the complex organization dealing with every facet of Southern Baptist life that we know it as today. In many respects the period 1890–1920 was the most significant period in the development of the Convention.

The time of troubles in the third and fourth decades of this century taught the Convention many lessons. Among the most important were those relating to the need for closer co-operation, more co-ordination, and greater efficiency. Consequently, out of these troublous days emerged a Convention in which emphasis upon growth, promotion, co-ordination, co-operation, efficiency, stewardship, and evangelism was characteristic.

Encouraging signs are the tremendous vitality of the Convention, the enlarging concept of evangelism, missions, and education, the increasing consciousness of the relevance of social issues, and the continuing unity of spirit within the Convention.

As lessons are gathered for the future, means must not be mistaken for ends. Organization, efficiency, promotion, physical property, size, all must be put in their relative place while the ends related to missions, evangelism, and education are kept in proper balance.

There is a need for Southern Baptists to become increasingly aware of the whole world in which they live and to reject provincialism or a limited outlook. This will demand continued strong and devoted leadership.

Southern Baptists must continue to be willing to be properly self-critical and to retain the flexibility of their program. Self-satisfaction and smugness are self-deceitful.

And finally, Southern Baptists must ever be mindful that the goal is the service of God who has manifested himself in Jesus Christ and who continues ever present as Holy Spirit. So long as they join the tripod of missions, evangelism, and education in the service of the Trinity of God, Southern Baptists will forge ahead.

SUGGESTED TOPICS FOR DISCUSSION

1. Discuss the factors which have made the years since 1944 such years of progress.
2. Discuss the problems attendant upon rapid growth.
3. Discuss the prospects for the Southern Baptist Convention.

QUESTIONS FOR REVIEW AND EXAMINATION

CONCERNING the examination and the requesting of awards, see Directions for the Teaching and the Study of This Book for Credit, page 147.

CHAPTER 1

1. How were Particular and General Baptists alike, and how did they differ?
2. Write briefly about the life and work of Roger Williams and John Clarke.
3. Who were the Separate Baptists? Describe them.

CHAPTER 2

4. What was the Great Kentucky Revival? Describe it and its influence.
5. Why were Baptists persecuted in Virginia?
6. What contributions did Oliver Hart and Richard Furman make to Baptist education?

CHAPTER 3

7. What is the difference between the "society" and "convention" methods of Baptist organization?
8. List reasons for the formation of the Southern Baptist Convention.
9. Identify the following men: James B. Taylor, Jeremiah B. Jeter, William B. Johnson, Basil Manly, Sr., and Francis Wayland.

CHAPTER 4

10. What was the first foreign mission field of the Southern Baptist Convention?
11. What great difficulties faced the Board of Domestic Missions at the beginning?
12. What was the Bible Board?
13. What was Landmarkism?

CHAPTER 5

14. How did I. T. Tichenor save the Board of Domestic Missions?
15. Why did the Southern Seminary move to Louisville?

CHAPTER 6

16. What is the relationship of Woman's Missionary Union to the Convention?
17. What was the Layman's Missionary Movement?
18. Who was the "father" of the Sunday School Board?
19. What is the purpose of the Baptist World Alliance?

CHAPTER 7

20. How much truth is there in the view that the Seventy-five Million Campaign was a failure?
21. What is the Executive Committee?
22. What was the Hundred Thousand Club?

CHAPTER 8

23. What is the Advance Program of Foreign Missions?
24. Name the top officers of the Foreign Mission Board, the Home Mission Board, the Sunday School Board, and each of the seminaries.
25. Comment on the future of Southern Baptists.

DIRECTIONS FOR THE TEACHING AND THE STUDY OF THIS BOOK FOR CREDIT

I. DIRECTIONS FOR THE TEACHER

1. Ten class periods of forty-five minutes each, or the equivalent, are required for the completion of this book for credit.

2. The teacher of the class will be given an award on the book if he requests it.

3. The teacher shall give a written examination covering the subject matter in the textbook, with at least one question or written assignment on each chapter, and the student shall make a minimum grade of 70 per cent. The written examination may take the form of assigned work to be done and written up between the class sessions, in the class sessions, or as a final written examination at the end of the course.

EXCEPTION: All who attend all of the class sessions, who read the book through by the close of the course, and who, in the judgment of the teacher, do the classwork satisfactorily may be exempted from taking the examination.

4. In the Graded Training Union Study Course, a seal for subject 10, The Denomination, is granted for the completion of this book.

Sunday school credit may be elected by Young People and Adults. Application for Sunday school awards should be sent to the state Sunday school department and for Training Union awards to the state Training Union department. These departments will provide the forms for these applications. They should be made in duplicate and both copies sent.

II. DIRECTIONS FOR THE STUDENT

1. *In Classwork*

(1) The pupil must attend at least 6 of the 10 forty-five minute periods to be eligible to take the class examination.

(2) The pupil who takes the class examination must certify that the textbook has been read. (In rare cases where pupils may find it impracticable to read the book before the completion of the classwork, the teacher may accept a promise to read the book carefully within the next two weeks.)

(3) The pupil must take a written examination, with at least one question or written assignment from each chapter, making

147

a minimum grade of 70 per cent. (All who attend all of the class sessions; who read the book through by the close of the course; and who, in the judgment of the teacher, do satisfactory classwork may be exempted from taking the examination.)

2. *In Individual Study by Correspondence*

Those who for any reason wish to study the book without the guidance of a teacher will use one of the following methods:

(1) Write the answers to the questions printed in the book, or

(2) Write a summary of each chapter or a development of the chapter outlines.

If the second method is used, the student will study the book and then with the open book write a summary of each chapter or a development of the chapter outlines.

In either case the student must read the book through.

Students may find profit in studying the text together, but where awards are requested, individual papers are required. Carbon copies or duplicates in any form cannot be accepted.

All written work done by such students on books for Sunday school credit should be sent to the state Sunday school secretary. All of such work done on books for Training Union credit should be sent to the state Training Union secretary.

III. INTERCHANGE OF CREDITS AND AWARDS ON COMPARABLE SUBJECTS

One award, either for Training Union or Sunday school, is granted for completing this book.

J. E. LAMBDIN
Secretary, Training Union Department
Baptist Sunday School Board

C. AUBREY HEARN
Director of the Study Course

BIBLIOGRAPHY

BAKER, ROBERT ANDREW. *Relations Between Northern and Southern Baptists*. Fort Worth: Seminary Hill Press, 1948. $3.00

BARNES, WILLIAM WRIGHT. *The Southern Baptist Convention 1845–1953*. Nashville: The Broadman Press, 1954. $3.75

COX, NORMAN W., ed. *Encyclopedia of Southern Baptists*. Nashville: Broadman Press, 1958. 2 vol., $16.50

DAWSON, JOSEPH MARTIN. *Baptists and the American Republic*. Nashville: Broadman Press, 1956. $3.00

MAGRUDER, EDITH CLYSDALE. *A Historical Study of the Educational Agencies of the Southern Baptist Convention, 1845–1945*. New York: Teachers College, Columbia University, 1951.

SWEET, WILLIAM WARREN. *The Story of Religion in America*. New York: Harper & Bros., 1950. $3.75

TORBET, ROBERT G. *The Baptist Ministry: Then and Now*. Philadelphia: The Judson Press, 1953. Pa. $1.25; Cl. $2.00

TORBET, ROBERT G. *The Baptist Story*. Philadelphia: The Judson Press, 1957. $1.50

TORBET, ROBERT G. *A History of the Baptists*. Philadelphia: The Judson Press, revised edition, 1955. $6.00

TORBET, ROBERT G. *Venture of Faith: The Story of the American Baptist Foreign Mission Society and the Woman's American Baptist Foreign Mission Society, 1814–1954*. Philadelphia: The Judson Press, 1955. $6.00

VEDDER, HENRY C. *A Short History of the Baptists*. Philadelphia: The Judson Press, 1907. $6.00

Notes

DATE DUE